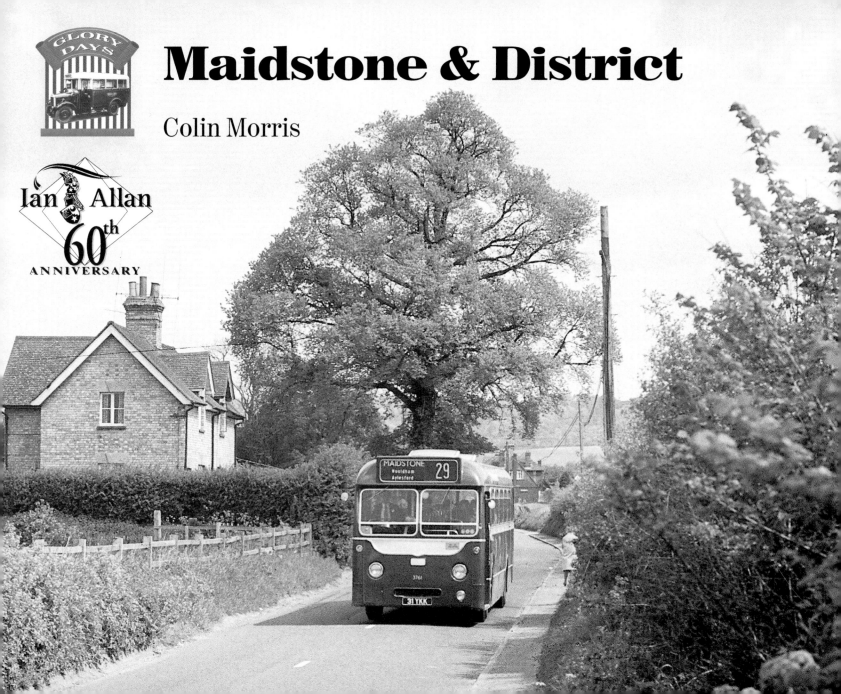

GLORY DAYS

Maidstone & District

Colin Morris

Ian Allan
60th
ANNIVERSARY

Front cover:
In delightful Winchelsea, Sussex, on 18 May 1974 is No 3403 (UKE 403H), a Leyland Leopard PSU4A/2R with Marshall 45-seat saloon bodywork. It was one of a batch of 20 delivered in dark Brunswick green and 'broken white' in 1970, most of which put in some 12 years' service with the company, latterly in NBC's leaf green. No 3403 was on service between Rye and Hastings, taking the southerly route between the two. *M. R. Hodges*

Back cover:
In NBC livery at the charmingly-preserved village of Speldhurst on 29 September 1978 is No 3466 (GKE 466L), a Leyland Leopard PSU4B/4R with Marshall bodywork. At that time, M&D services were operated from here to Tunbridge Wells and Hawkhurst or Ashford with some 20 departures on weekdays. These passed through villages which epitomised the rural aspect of Maidstone & District's work in its glory days. *M. R. Hodges*

Title page:
Much of Maidstone & District's territory lay across some of the most fertile countryside in the United Kingdom. Eccles — 'the meadow of the oak' — looks part of it, but it was better-known for its quarries rather than agricultural produce. Nevertheless, an AEC Reliance/ Willowbrook saloon completes a rather pretty picture there in May 1973. However, most of M&D's revenue came from work in urban areas. *M. R. Hodges*

Contents

For Jan Bannister

First published 2002

ISBN 0 7110 2858 3

© Colin Morris 2002

Published by Ian Allan Publishing

an imprint of Ian Allan Publishing Ltd, Hersham, Surrey KT12 4RG.
Printed by Ian Allan Printing Ltd, Hersham, Surrey KT12 4RG.

Code: 0207/B2

Foreword

I knew little about M&D and Kent until, on St David's Day 1977, I arrived at the company in Chatham. I had this vision of a rural operation, green buses wandering through apple orchards and hop gardens once every second Tuesday, carrying folk to market. From afar, I wondered why they needed all those double-decks. I was certainly not prepared to find a basically urban operator — almost a municipal — covering the Medway Towns (a conurbation bigger than Southampton), Tunbridge Wells and Tonbridge, and the major operator in the Maidstone area. Linking these, despite an intensive railway operation, were busy inter-urban routes. Yes, there were rural parts, but these were not what M&D was principally about.

M&D — *the* M&D — was a household name in its market. Fleet livery had changed to NBC green, but green it still was, and — dare I say it — one that wore a lot better than the old, darker shade. And what a fleet it was! Already varied, it was chosen to evaluate different types by NBC, and all manner of things arrived. Used to different types, we began to build up a select fleet of second-hand purchases that ensured interest and variety galore.

But a company is not about colours and buses, and where they go; it's about people. It's a people industry. Latterly, we carried 21 million people a year and employed 975 people to do it. That's what it's all about. What struck me about M&D when I joined was that everyone felt part of it — and it, in turn, was felt to be part of the communities it served. I tried to foster that, and today people still refer to the old firm with fondness.

I am delighted to be associated with Colin's lovely book about 'the M&D'.

Roger Davies
Linton, Kent, 2002

Acknowledgements

In 1974, Len Higgins, at the time Chief General Manager of NBC's Kent Division, asked me to write a book about Maidstone & District Motor Services Ltd. He set aside George French's old green-topped desk at Knightrider House as a work-station and introduced me to Stan Wicks, the diligent keeper of the company archives. In turn, Stan arranged interviews with several people whose connections with M&D went back many years. Among them were Mrs George French, Mrs Oscar Pritchard, Alfred Kelcey, R. Don Marshall, Brian Reeves, Jack E. Baker, Ernest J. Fowler, Harry Redstall, Albert G. Ingerfield, Sidney Wainwright, Horace 'Freddie' Fridd, George A. Finn, Ernest W. Pynn and Robert J. Eacott. I had valuable correspondence with Mrs E. French, the daughter of A. W. Austen, and her grand-daughter Gillian Dunmall. I wrote a 50,000-word history which was painstakingly perused over many years by Nicholas King, Bob Cook and David Padgham, and the saga of why that material has not been published would make a book of its own. It is thus with considerable relief that, courtesy of Ian Allan Publishing Ltd, I may now present a somewhat shorter version in the 'Glory Days' series. Amazingly, for a company the size of M&D, this is the first case-bound book devoted to it.

More recently, Nicholas King provided introductions to three key figures. First, Stephen Trennery, ex-Chairman and Managing Director of M&D, kindly checked the appropriate sections. Roger Davies, ex-Director of Operations, without whom — well, anyone who knows him realises what a mine of information he is, freely given, at great length and with enormous enthusiasm and generosity. Then there was Richard E. Rosa, the most scholarly researcher into transport history I have had the good fortune to meet; I am most grateful to him for permission to quote from his works (see Further Reading) and for checking my manuscript.

I am similarly very grateful to Kevin Hawkins, Commercial Director of Arriva Southern Counties, for granting me an interview at Invicta House, Maidstone.

For illustrations, I have been fortunate to have access to the colour slides taken by Mike Hodges, Senior Public Transport Planner at Kent County Council, and to the ticket collection of Andrew Waller of the Transport Ticket Society. Black-and-white prints were kindly provided from the collections of Alan Lambert, Alan Townsin, R. H. Hannay, Richard Rosa and the Ian Allan Library. Additional research was undertaken on my behalf by the staff of Bexhill Library and by Richard Lewis at Maidstone.

Colin Morris
Heswall, April 2002

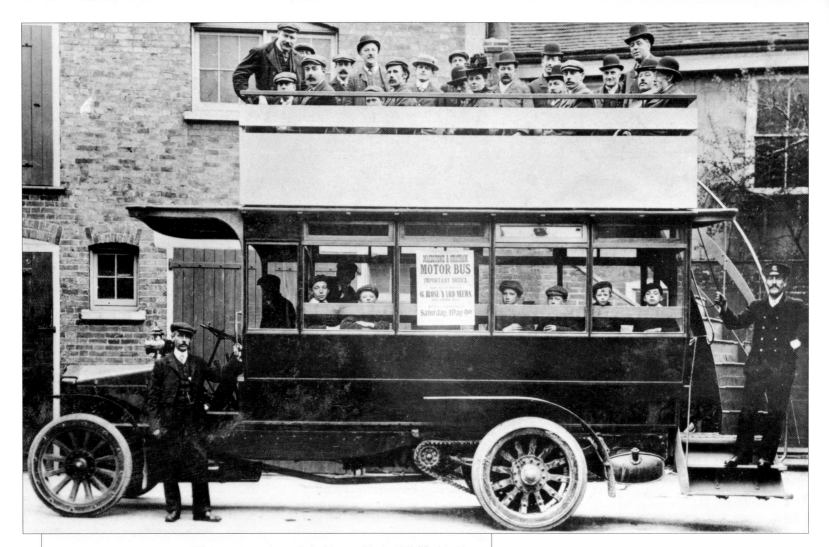

▲ William Austen stands proudly beside a varnished-teak Hallford double-decker (D 3801) of his Commercial Motor Co at 6 Rose Yard Mews, Maidstone. In company with Darracq-Serpollet LN 6031, this Dartford-built motorbus commenced a passenger service to Chatham on Saturday 9 May 1908, via Lower and Upper Bell. The single fare was originally 6d (2½p), one half of the corresponding railway fare. *Colin Morris collection*

1. Foundations

Save the odd blemish, Kent is an attractive county, and Maidstone, its administrative centre, is but a short distance from countryside which William Cobbett called 'the finest I have ever seen in all England'. Maidstone, 'the town on the River Medway', sits practically astride the main road and rail links between London and Folkestone, whilst the river itself wends its way northward through a gap in the North Downs to its large tidal estuary. Here it supported the growth of Chatham, Gillingham and the City of Rochester, now themselves known collectively as 'Medway'.

Railways began to arrive in the area in 1844, but the line from Maidstone to Rochester went up the west bank of the river. It was over half a century later that a proposal for a more direct inter-urban electric tramway between Maidstone and Chatham was authorised by an Act of Parliament, in 1903. Yet, though the Chatham & District Light Railways Co and Maidstone Corporation established electric tramways in the respective towns, the approved tramway between the two was never built. Thus the way was left clear for the provision of a motorbus service.

Official brochures touching upon the early history of Maidstone & District Motor Services Ltd do not bend over backwards to explain that, although that important pioneer of the motorbus industry, Walter Flexman French, set up the company, his was not the initiative which established the first proper motorbus service between Maidstone and Chatham. Credit for that belongs to a Maidstone resident, William Austen (1863–1930). Born near Brenchley in the Weald, Austen worked in the drapery business and as a salesman, moving on to provide a service delivering locally-grown fruit to London by road. On the return trip he brought national newspapers in time for breakfast-table delivery — a service surprisingly neglected by the South Eastern and London, Chatham & Dover railway companies. At the age of 44 he decided to try his hand at road passenger transport, arranging for a Darracq-Serpollet steam bus to make a trial run from London to Maidstone in February 1908 along what became the A20.

William Austen formed the Commercial Motor Co and hired the steam bus for further trips to London and excursions and private-hire work. On 9 May 1908, in the company of a Hallford motorbus, he placed it in regular service between Maidstone and Chatham for a period of one month, after which it was returned to Darracq-Serpollet. The competitive trial had been won by the

Hallford, and Austen chose to purchase two additional examples from the manufacturer on the hire-purchase system. Harry Austin, the first driver employed by CMC, did not experience any trouble with the Hallfords, despite the long climb on Blue Bell Hill. From July 1908 a second route to Chatham went along the Medway valley via Aylesford, Wouldham and Rochester — a distance of 14 miles. A third service was operated briefly in Maidstone between Boxley Road, North Ward and the Athletic Ground. A garage was rented in Week Street, and bookings were made at Bennit's the newsagents in Maidstone High Street.

In addition to experiments with registration-plate designs and methods of illuminating them, Austen fitted at least one of the Hallfords with waterproof stormsheets on the open top deck — two layers of fabric bonded to rubber, which could be pulled up from the floor on a roller-blind principle. This then went over the passengers' shoulders and was attached to the rear of the seat. It worked well enough, but rough handling put paid to that.

On 27 February 1908 a Darracq-Serpollet double-decker steam bus made a trial run from London to Maidstone, 'spurting over the steepest portions of the famous hill at Wrotham at good speed'. LN 6031 was probably that vehicle. It was photographed, whilst on trial with the Commercial Motor Co of Maidstone, during an excursion to Hampton Court and back, on 27 June 1908. *Colin Morris collection*

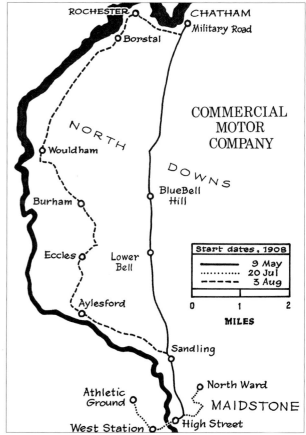

COMMERCIAL
MOTOR
COMPANY

Start dates, 1908

————	9 May
··········	20 Jul
– – – –	3 Aug

0   1   2
MILES

▲ After a month's trial the Darracq-Serpollet was returned to its maker, and William Austen acquired two more Hallfords (D 3943/4), on hire-purchase basis, from the manufacturer, J. & E. Hall Ltd of Dartford. Both were painted in a green and white livery and, together with D 3801, formed the established CMC fleet, which was particularly successful during the August Bank Holiday period in 1908. *Mrs E. French (daughter of A. W. Austen)*

Generally, the Hallfords were trouble-free until overcome by the elements. No one enjoyed travelling on the top deck in the rain, and in the poor light of dusk a bus could go across the grass verge and into a ditch very easily. Although no one was injured, there were insufficient vehicles to send out a spare, leading to great inconvenience. The company's support and income began to flag, and Austen's financial resources could no longer cope.

By the end of 1908, CMC could not meet the repayments and the manufacturer of the three buses, J. & E. Hall Ltd, took out a summons. Austen decided to defend himself in court — and in the morning's session he was eloquent and well received. He repaired to a local hostelry for lunch and a premature celebration, and it speaks volumes for the man that he disclosed to family and friends that he returned considerably less sharp than before. J. & E. Hall repossessed the three Hallfords on 19 March 1909.

Rather than leave the Maidstone and Chatham road unserved, J. & E. Hall decided to employ the road crews itself and to enlarge the fleet. On 21 June 1909 the firm put on a new route between Chatham and Gravesend, after which it called the

enterprise the 'Maidstone, Chatham and Gravesend Omnibus Service'. Pioneer road-transport historian Charles E. Lee recorded in 1962 that the Halls appointed a Mr Sadler to act as Manager. On 26 June, however, a Hallford knocked down and killed a 13-year-old youth in Chatham — and from that date the company was actively looking for a purchaser. It was at this point that W. F. French made a formal offer for the undertaking in his own name, the deal being finalised in May 1910.

Walter Flexman French (1856–1925) was born in Springfield, Chelmsford, as Walter Flexman. Of small stature but possessing considerable charm and wit, he was very much a self-made man. Said to have been apprenticed to the London, Chatham & Dover

Railway Co and to have spent 14 years 'in charge' in locomotive shops, in June 1888 he nevertheless set up shop as the South Road Cycle Co at Balham, where he built and sold bicycles. Around this time he added 'French' to his name 'to conceal the fact that he was running a private business while in railway employment', suggested Charles Lee in 1968. Writing to Lee in 1938, Douglas Mackenzie (of Southdown fame) referred to French's 'South Western Motor Car Co Ltd', which started running a service of MMC and Daimler wagonettes from Streatham to Clapham Junction in 1901: 'The old gentleman used to say that his was the first service in London, but I knew that he was not too accurate in these sort of things.' Not surprising then, that many have remained convinced that M&D started in 1908. Nevertheless, this was all part of the 'charm' and, in the late 'Teens and early 'Twenties of the 20th century, French became one of the 'movers and shakers' of the emergent motor-omnibus industry, becoming Chairman of Devon General, Hants & Dorset, Southdown and, of course, Maidstone & District, as well as taking a leading role in the founding of several other such firms.

In order that French could return to London to develop his car-hire business into French's Garage & Motor Works Ltd (which later became the United Service Transport Co Ltd, one of the largest goods and passenger transport firms in the United Kingdom), on 6 August 1910 he presented his elder son George with an unusual birthday present. Giving up a post with London & District, George Flexman French arrived in Maidstone to take up the post of Operating Manager and Engineer at a salary of 55 shillings (£2.75) per week and, as his first wife Minnie said at the time, 'leaving a good job in London and

coming down here; there must be something wrong with your brain!' There is little doubt that George French expected a free hand to run the Maidstone, Chatham and Gravesend services as he pleased. That may have been the case during the first six months or so, but his father had bigger ideas. Walter Flexman French decided, for the first time, to employ a strategy which would be repeated as he set up omnibus companies elsewhere — to go into partnership with a locally-based colleague with sufficient capital or resources to provide each enterprise with a healthy kick-start. At Maidstone that man was landowner, huntsman and civil engineer Humphrey Robinson, of the Manor House, Sundridge, Sevenoaks. Together they began to plan the infrastructure of one of the first provincial 'territorial' companies with agreed boundaries, three years before such inter-company agreements began to come into fashion. Like it or not, George French was to become answerable to first one and then the other of the founding duo of Maidstone & District for over 34 years.

George French's description of his adopted fleet was 'the most primitive thing I ever came to', epitomised, perhaps, by the day in September 1910 when he had to deal with an unusual accident. One of the Hallfords went into a side-slip on the Chatham road, and, in the resulting impact, three of the seven passengers injured had to be detained in hospital. George's solution was simple: he told his father, who came down from London with a large bag of silver and paid the claimants on the spot. There was, therefore, no recourse to litigation or insurance, and no apparent loss of custom for the service. In addition, George arranged for Maidstone Borough and Chatham Town councils to inspect his buses alternately every six months, thereby

◄◄ The three stage-carriage services pioneered by William Austen (who added an 'A' in the belief that 'A. W.' Austen sounded more businesslike), those to Chatham laying the foundations for the establishment of Maidstone & District Motor Services Ltd in 1911. That between the west and north wards of Maidstone failed to attract sufficient public support and was consequently withdrawn after a mere 10 days.
Colin Morris collection

◄ Walter Flexman French, pioneer and founder of several motorbus companies in the South of England. When the Commercial Motor Co's vehicles were repossessed by J. & E. Hall Ltd in March 1909, the latter continued to run the service but sought a purchaser. Enter in May 1910 W. F. French, who added a route to West Malling and based his fleet at premises in a yard off St Peter's Street, Maidstone.
Colin Morris collection

◄ The Maidstone & District Motor Services Ltd was registered as a new company on 22 March 1911, with a capital of £4,000. Half of that amount was invested by Humphrey Ingram Robinson, later Colonel of the Queen's Own Royal West Kent Regiment. He became General Manager and then Chairman of Maidstone & District until his death in March 1945. In the company also, he had always been referred to by his military rank. *Colin Morris collection*

From the very beginning in 1910, Walter Flexman French had encountered some opposition upon the road to Chatham. Thomas Attree, founder of Road Motors Ltd, later based at Luton, Bedfordshire, appeared on the Maidstone–Chatham route with a grey-liveried Milnes-Daimler saloon bus (D 5317). Despite a spell running instead at Margate and an apparent withdrawal to Luton, when M&D paid Attree £302 10s 0d in September 1911 the purchase included this vehicle — although it seems somehow to have been handed back to Attree.
Alan Lambert collection

halving the time his vehicles would be inoperative and reducing the administrative work of both his firm and the local authorities. He had given notice of his major strength and contribution to the company which was about to be formed — a good eye for the thoroughly practical solution to problems as and when they arose, even if that meant bringing in someone with greater 'clout' to add the finishing touch.

Maidstone & District Motor Services Ltd was registered with company number 114841 on 22 March 1911, with a nominal capital of £4,000. Among the bet-hedging purposes listed in its Memorandum of Association were:

3(b) To carry on the business of motor jobmasters, motor omnibus, cab and other private or public conveyance proprietors; motor omnibus, charabanc, lorry and other vehicle manufacturers and repairers; garage, garage builders and dealers in motor spirit, lubricating oil and accessories in all their respective branches.

3(c) To manufacture, buy, sell, exchange, alter or improve and deal in vehicles of any kind whether constructed so as to progress by means of automatic power, steam, gas, electricity, hot air, alcohol, petrol, paraffin, or by any other fuel or agency whatever.

3(d) To carry on the business of carriers, motor car maintainers, mechanical engineers, machinists, fitters, wheelwrights, millwrights, dealers in oils, grease lubricating or otherwise, founders, wire-drawers, tube-makers, metallurgists, saddlers, galvanisers, japanners, annealers, enamellers, electroplaters, brass workers, painters, varnishers, vulcanisers, rubber merchants, tyre-makers, leather workers, tanners, packing-case makers, ticket makers and punch manufacturers, printers, advertisers, and generally to carry on any other business (albeit manufacturing or otherwise) which may be seen to the company capable of being conveniently carried on in connection with the above . . .

The Maidstone & District Motor Services, Ltd.,
HAULAGE CONTRACTORS.

Telephone: 257 MAIDSTONE.

MAIDSTONE,

191___

BOOKING OFFICES.
6, High Street, Maidstone.
Telephone 257.

4, Military Road, Chatham.
Telephone 465.

Ref............. Dicᵈ.........Typ..........

MAIDSTONE & DISTRICT MOTOR SERVICES Lᵀᴰ
HAULAGE CONTRACTORS,
Sᵀ PETERS STREET, MAIDSTONE.

◄ As this letterhead emphasises, haulage work was an important aspect of the fledgling company's work.
In addition to 'Motor Omnibuses, Pullmans and Torpedo Char-a-bancs for Private Parties and Excursions', there were 'Motor Lorries, open or closed, for rapid and direct transport of Furniture and Perishable Goods of all descriptions. . .'
Richard Rosa collection

◄ . . . as illustrated by the accompanying photograph of D 3449, one of French's earliest Hallfords. Its bus body has been removed from the 1907-vintage chassis and replaced by a tail-gated open truck, made ready for a night run to London with that Kentish speciality — a light but cumbersome load of freshly-picked and bagged hops.
Colin Morris collection

From the outset, French and Robinson foresaw the employment of a large and varied workforce which would be concerned with a great deal of in-house productivity.

As with many new firms, the beginning was rather more humble. The original Company Secretary, Herbert Paten, had as his office a very small wooden shed, where on a winter's morning the ink froze in the pots and the oil heater stifled the occupants. For security reasons the day's takings were hidden in a waste-paper basket. In 1912 A. E. Leaney was appointed Clerk and Cashier, and secretarial work was taken on by Humphrey Robinson. He was not the kind to suffer discomfort in a shed. His original role was to act as General Manager, whilst George French was responsible for the operational side of the business — the Garage Manager. The initial fleet placed in his care consisted of five Hallfords.

Those were the days when body-swaps were commonplace on public-service vehicles; charabancs became double-deckers overnight and *vice versa*. When necessary, some Hallfords doubled-up as tilt-cover, flatbed or drop-sided lorries taking timber, hops or Sharp's toffees on nightly trips to London, or with what the company called 'fruit crates' for local produce — the lorry bodies built by Dunk's of Milton Street, Maidstone. For the first 10 years or so the wages of fitters and other garage staff were in excess of those paid to the 'button staff', as drivers and conductors came to be known — probably to reflect their contribution to the 'haulage contractors' side of the business.

In order to establish Maidstone & District upon a more secure financial footing, Walter Flexman French consulted the British Electric Traction Co Ltd. BET, set up to establish electric tramways

Hallford D 4501 was first registered to J. & E. Hall Ltd on 10 June 1909 as a 'walnut' charabanc, and was probably one of the vehicles in Maidstone & District's opening fleet. The tail-heavy bodywork is a shallower version of the 'observation type' beloved of Douglas Mackenzie (of later Southdown fame), although the canvas canopy and its supports look uncharacteristically makeshift. *Alan Lambert collection*

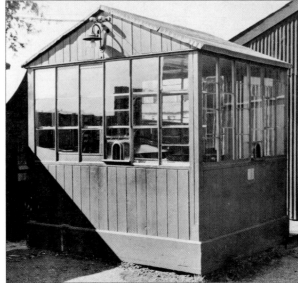

This small wooden-framed greenhouse-cum-shed was the company's first 'Head Office'. It originally stood in the yard at St Peter's Street, Maidstone, where it was described by those who manned it as 'freezing in winter and boiling in summer'. Conductors paid in through the small arched apertures, and the day's takings were hidden in a waste-paper basket. The hut was later restored and spent many years in the forecourt of Postley Works. *Colin Morris collection*

in the provinces, had been convinced by Sidney Garcke, son of one of its founders, Emile Garcke, that motorbuses could prove a useful adjunct to its business. Accordingly, a subsidiary, the British Automobile Traction Co Ltd, had been formed. BAT was in the process of ordering a fleet of new Daimler buses for use in London and elsewhere. French was thus able to use the good offices of BET to obtain favourable terms, and the benefits of an emergent War Office subsidy scheme, as part of M&D's order for the make.

On 31 May 1913 BET announced its intention to take a financial interest in M&D, and the capital was raised to £15,000. The following month, Sidney Garcke and William S. Wreathall joined the board as BET representatives, and Humphrey Robinson became Managing Director. Walter Flexman French remained Chairman, but George French soldiered on in his previous role.

Since (until 1921) M&D was now virtually a subsidiary of BET, that company's Brunswick (dark) green, lined out in gold and silver with small overlapping 'fern shoots' at the corners, was set to become the new standardised colour scheme. Saloon buses had roofs in 'broken white'. Whereas several companies wore the same livery initially, by the late 'Twenties all save Maidstone &

District had abandoned it, such that (minus the lining-out) it eventually became known as 'Maidstone & District Green' and 'Broken White' (formula in Docker's paint 3239, 2440 and 3239, 0350 respectively) — until the National Bus Company began to replace it with leaf green and white in 1972.

The registered office of M&D removed to a new garage and offices at Upper Stone Street on 22 April 1914, and eight days later the share capital was raised to £25,000. The company cost ledger shows that during the previous month the fleet comprised 5 Hallford, 1 Leyland, 18 Daimler and 8 Tilling-Stevens chassis. By the summer of 1914, there were services daily from Maidstone to Chatham, Faversham, Mereworth (for Tunbridge Wells) and Hastings (and on weekdays to Hawkhurst and Sevenoaks) and daily from Chatham to Gravesend and to Sittingbourne.

Upon the outbreak of World War 1 in August 1914, four Hallfords and 11 of the relatively new Daimlers were requisitioned for military use, some with M&D drivers selected for war service. Only the chassis were taken, several of the bodies being stored at rented accommodation in Faversham, initially. In 1915 the company managed to match that loss by adding 15 replacement vehicles largely of makes the Army did not want, plus a Daimler which the staff at Upper Stone Street built up from spare parts. Among the new and untried types were Caledon, Commer, Ensign, Romar and Straker-Squire chassis, several fitted with previously-stored bodywork. Body repairs were undertaken at newly-acquired premises in Fox Street, Gillingham, and some painting was done in a garage at Sutton Valence.

George French designed electric-lighting sets to replace acetylene

11

The motley colours which adorned M&D's early vehicles gradually disappeared after June 1913, when the British Electric Traction Co Ltd took an interest and two of its directors joined the board. D 9717, a 40hp Leyland with what was described as a 'Pullman saloon body' by Christopher Dodson, was probably the first to be painted in BET's dark Brunswick green livery in anticipation of this large increase in capital. *Alan Lambert collection*

In BET dark green and 'broken-white' livery is a Daimler 40hp model, thought to be KT 516, with bodywork built in Birch Bros style by the Brush Electrical Engineering Co Ltd at Loughborough — a BET associate company. The 'full-title' standard fleetname used until 1919 is unusual on this example in that all the letters are of the same height, and the Brush signwriter has demonstrated his skill by adding serifs. *Richard Rosa collection*

▲ The Maidstone & District yard at St Peter's Street was the setting
for an official photograph of three vehicles delivered in 1913.
KT 269 was a Tilling-Stevens with TTA2-style radiator which had
been working the Staplehurst and Cranbrook service, whilst
KT 873/4 were 40hp Daimlers. The latter appear unused and, since
they were delivered that November, this probably dates the
picture. All three were bodied by Birch.
M. R. Hodges collection

KT 965, a Daimler B and the last vehicle delivered in 1913, pauses at 'The George' in Sittingbourne High Street *en route* to Faversham along Watling Street, which became the A2. In 1915 the Maidstone–Sittingbourne–Faversham route was lettered 'C'. When the letters ran out it became service 3, and survives to this day as the 333 — a delightful link with days of yore.
Richard Rosa collection

systems in the buses and considered alternative fuels after Government-imposed petrol rationing. Town gas was the chosen solution, although few buses were so equipped, and the exercise was never fully satisfactory. A half-deflated gas bag strapped to the roof was always at the mercy of strong winds. E. C. Tong, at the time a 5s-per-week (25p) apprentice mechanic, recalled one coming off on the Hadlow road and that he had to climb a tree to recover it. Elsewhere, bus crews chased escaped gas bags across fields, to 'the great merriment among the passengers'. The last gas bag was removed from a Tilling-Stevens in the summer of 1918.

On 24 January 1916 Ernest Neve of Sutton Valence sold his Reliance Motor Services, three Leyland saloons and garages at Tenterden and Sutton Valence to M&D for £1,000, and became a shareholder. Additionally M&D entered into a no-competition agreement with C. & J. Bennett of Tenterden — the proud operator of the last horse-bus to run into Maidstone, who had turned to motor traction merely to cope with competition from Ernest Neve. The arrangement was to last for a considerable number of years, providing M&D with parking space at

Tenterden and Bennetts with a big brother in the competitive stakes. Otherwise, the company decided to combat rival operators during World War 1 with more-frequent journeys and reduced fares.

Although war curtailed much expansion of the motorbus industry, it did not stop managements from thinking about the subject. Just how far geographically should each company go? Maidstone & District already had an informal agreement for the protection of its northwestern flank. In 1914 Walter Flexman French met Arthur Hawkins, Managing Director of the East Surrey Traction Co Ltd (founded just six days before M&D), and came to a settlement. Their common border was a line drawn from Sevenoaks, Eynsford and Farningham, along the Darent Valley to the south bank of the Thames at Dartford.

A more leisurely approach to demarcation was necessary on the southern and eastern flanks, because Southdown and East Kent did not come into being until 1915 and 1916 respectively. A memorandum of mutual agreement with those companies was approved on 5 July 1917. Basically, Maidstone & District territory comprised Kent and Sussex east of a line drawn Hailsham–Tunbridge Wells–Tonbridge–Sevenoaks (and to the Thames at Dartford); west of a line drawn from The Swale due north of Faversham Town Hall, straight to Faversham, then Ashford–Hamstreet–Appledore and the Isle of Oxney to Rye, Winchelsea and Hastings; and north of a line eastward along the main road from Hailsham and thence along the east side of the main road from Battle to Hastings, thus (at this stage) leaving Bexhill, Ninfield and Hooe in proposed Southdown territory. At the same time, M&D agreed to East Kent's picking up and setting down passengers at Hothfield, three miles northwest of Ashford, in consideration of commission payments.

Although Percival Graefe had become Company Secretary in 1916, George French's elevation to on-the-spot decision-maker (since Robinson had gone off to war) now obliged him to deal with official correspondence. Thus Kitty Redstall became his first Private Secretary — and the first woman about the place as well. Lady cleaners appeared in the Upper Stone Street offices, and clerks who could type and do Pitman's shorthand were engaged, as were conductresses to replace men conscripted for war service — a saving, because they accepted lower wages.

Nevertheless, the needs of the military, munition and construction workers were nowhere large enough to compensate for the loss of civilian traffic — the severe rationing of fuel saw to that. This is borne out by the net profits gained during the

Vehicles were still being delivered in red/blue, red/black and red/white liveries in 1914, but most arrived in BET dark green. Among them were four Tilling-bodied Tilling-Stevens TS3 saloons. KT 1911 was the first, delivered that April, and is seen on the Wateringbury and Mereworth service. The lady passenger's elbow resting upon the beading trim shows that this type had full-drop windows. *Richard Rosa collection*

The outbreak of World War 1 resulted in the War Office requisition of several vehicles. As elsewhere, Maidstone & District was obliged to replace them with whatever make of chassis the military did not want. Among them in 1915 was this Straker-Squire CO5 with Tilling bodywork built in that firm's Wren Road factory in Camberwell (KT 6415). The Chatham–Maidstone route has become 'A' in a newly-lettered series. *Alan Townsin collection*

St Peter's. Rochester.
Outing to Brighton July 8th 1919

▲ On 24 January 1916 Maidstone & District purchased the goodwill, plant,
machinery and three Leyland saloon buses of Ernest Neve's Reliance
Motor Services, based at Sutton Valence. The most modern was a 40hp
saloon of 1914 with a body by Leyland. On 8 July 1919 it was hired
by the vicar and parishioners of St Peter's Church, Rochester, for an
outing to Brighton, possibly in celebration of that first postwar summer.
Alan Lambert collection

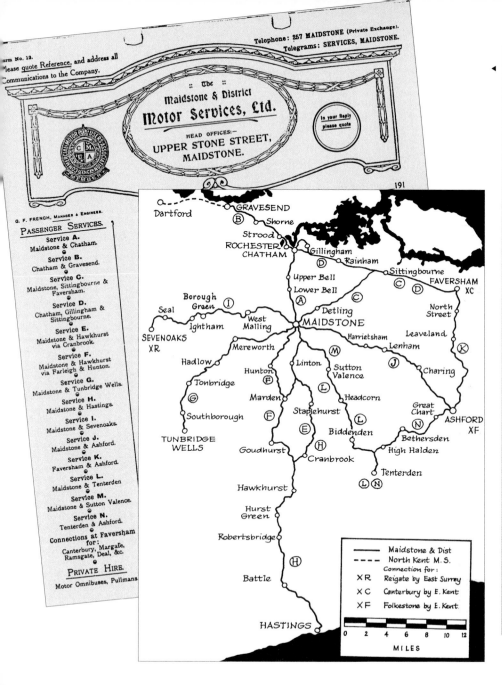

Form No. 12.

Please quote Reference, and address all Communications to the Company.

Telephone: 257 MAIDSTONE (Private Exchange).
Telegrams: SERVICES, MAIDSTONE.

:: The ::
Maidstone & District
Motor Services, Ltd.

HEAD OFFICES:—
UPPER STONE STREET,
MAIDSTONE.

In your Reply please quote

G. F. FRENCH, MANAGER & ENGINEER.

PASSENGER SERVICES.

Service A.
Maidstone & Chatham.

Service B.
Chatham & Gravesend.

Service C.
Maidstone, Sittingbourne & Faversham.

Service D.
Chatham, Gillingham & Sittingbourne.

Service E.
Maidstone & Hawkhurst via Cranbrook.

Service F.
Maidstone & Hawkhurst via Farleigh & Hunton.

Service G.
Maidstone & Tunbridge Wells.

Service H.
Maidstone & Hastings.

Service I.
Maidstone & Sevenoaks.

Service J.
Maidstone & Ashford.

Service K.
Faversham & Ashford.

Service L.
Maidstone & Tenterden

Service M.
Maidstone & Sutton Valence.

Service N.
Tenterden & Ashford.

Connections at Faversham for:
Canterbury, Margate, Ramsgate, Deal, &c.

PRIVATE HIRE.

Motor Omnibuses, Pullmans.

Map legend:

— Maidstone & Dist
‑ ‑ ‑ North Kent M.S.
Connection for:
X R   Reigate by East Surrey
X C   Canterbury by E. Kent
X F   Folkestone by E. Kent

0 2 4 6 8 10 12
MILES

In 1915 the company decided to identify its routes with a series of code letters. The map shows those services inaugurated by March 1916 — service 'N' being the last introduced during World War 1. Service 'G' went only as far as Mereworth, where Autocar Services Ltd of Tunbridge Wells provided the connecting link, and it would appear that service 'B' was worked jointly with 'North Kent' buses. Service 'O', Hastings–Eastbourne, was not added until June 1919. *Colin Morris collection*

Since there was no fleet intake during the last two years (1917/18) of World War 1, it is likely that the 18 vehicles received with open arms in 1919 were the first to carry the famous Maidstone & District scroll fleetname upon their BET dark Brunswick-green livery. Among them was KN 2405, a Leyland N saloon with Harrington bodywork, at work on the Maidstone–Hastings service — fully reinstated in February 1919 after wartime suspension. *M&D and East Kent Bus Club*

Whereas, in the early days, some other bus companies permitted crew members to carry and charge for parcels and packages (and pocket whatever they received for that service as 'perks'), Maidstone & District had a properly scaled pre-paid system from the outset. In the summer of 1916, however, some services were suspended completely as World War 1 increased its stranglehold upon both men and materials. It was not until 1919 that the company was able to reinstate them all.
Colin Morris collection

formative first decade, beginning with £145 in 1911/12 (World War 1: 1914–18):

1913	£1,626	9s	7d
1914	£5,841	10s	0d
1915	£12,082	5s	10d
1916	£9,428	8s	0d
1917	£6,129	13s	0d
1918	£7,573	18s	0d
1919	£8,486	13s	3d
1920	£15,422	2s	1d

The 1915 figure includes the best part of five months' peacetime operation, the 1919 figure four months'. By 1922 the profit margin had risen to £34,396 13s 3d, which gives a fair indication of what the war cost the company in financial terms.

As M&D went on to absorb the operations of other operators — tramways in particular — it inherited the loyalty of numerous other people, engineering, maintenance, office and button-staff. But there was always a tacit understanding that there was something special about those who laid the foundations of M&D: people like Wally Smith the bus washer, G. C. Grimes the fitter, drivers Bill Blackman, W. T. Philpott, G. Baker, F. C. Mitchell and 'Freddie Fridd', conductors Jenner and J. Kennedy and George French's cousin Walter J. Flexman, who had helped out at Maidstone.

(Service **N**)

TENTERDEN and ASHFORD.
WEEK DAYS AND SUNDAYS (EXCEPT WEDNESDAYS).

NOTICE.

Owing to the very great shortage in labour and the restrictions in supplies, the Company very much regret to announce that they have been compelled to suspend this Service until further notice. Notice will be given immediately it is possible to resume same.

SEND YOUR PARCELS BY MOTOR BUS.   Quickest and Cheapest means of conveying Parcels.
For Rates, &c., see page 24.

East Kent Road Car Company's, and the East Surrey Traction Company's Time Tables may be obtained at any of this Company's Booking Offices.

Connections at Sevenoaks with the East Surrey Traction Company's Services for Oxted, Redhill, Reigate, &c.

PARCEL RATES.
WEIGHT NOT EXCEEDING :

Penny Fare Stages	2 lbs	3 lbs	4 lbs	5 lbs	6 lbs	7 lbs	14 lbs	21 lbs	28 lbs	35 lbs	49 lbs	56 lbs
Not exceeding 10 ...	3d.	3d.	3d.	3d.	3d.	3d.	4d.	5d.	6d.	7d.	8d.	9d
Not exceeding 15 ...	3	3	3	3	4	4	5	6	7	8	9	10
Not exceeding 20 ...	3	3	3	4	5	5	6	7	8	9	10	11
Not exceeding 25 ...	3	3	4	5	6	6	7	8	9	10	11	1/-
Not exceeding 30 ...	3	4	5	6	7	7	8	9	10	11	1/-	1/1
Not exceeding 35 ...	4	5	6	7	8	8	9	10	11	1/-	1/1	1/2

PARCEL & PASSENGER BOOKING OFFICES.

Maidstone—Bennitt's, Cannon. Bennitt's, High St.
Chatham—Mrs. Taverner, 4, Military Road.
Sittingbourne—The Bull Hotel.
Ashford—Masters, 48, High St.
Gravesend—Company's Office, New Road.

*Sutton Val.—W. G. Russell, King's Head.
Tenterden—Bennett's, W Crs.
Hastings—Watson's, Harold Place.
*Biddenden—Rose Inn.

*Headcorn—George Hotel.
*Goudhurst—The Vine.
*Stockbury—The Squirrels.
*Faversham—F. Skinner, 41, Court Street.
*W. Malling—H. C. H. Oliver.
*Marden—W. Starr.

* **Parcels only.**

2. Territorial Development

The armistice of November 1918 which put an end to World War 1 did not bring about an immediate improvement in the bus industry. For instance, it took a great deal of lobbying at local level — well into 1919 — to get the Petrol Control Department of the Board of Trade to increase the allowance of fuel granted for passenger services. Significantly, service 'O', the first addition to M&D's lettered system since the war, did not start running between Hastings and Eastbourne until 28 June 1919, followed by service 'P' between Tenterden and Hastings on 19 January 1920. A service from Hawkhurst to Lewes, planned as 'Q', became instead service 18, a Southdown-series number adopted by M&D for a joint service with that company right through to Brighton. After a Tilling-Stevens TS3 delivered at the end of 1916, the next new vehicles did not become available until April 1919. Between then and August, six more Tilling-Stevens and an AEC joined the fleet, together with the first 10 of an eventual 38

Leyland N chassis — saloon bodies by Tilling and by Dodson, charabancs by Harrington. All the wartime emergency chassis had gone by 1920, when 15 additional Tilling-Stevens, the next batch of 21 Leyland N and the first two long-chassised Leyland O types were added. The share capital had been raised to £150,000 in January of that year.

Gravesend and Dartford

BET had purchased the horse-drawn Gravesend, Rosherville & Northfleet Tramways Co Ltd in January 1901 and reconstructed it as the Gravesend & Northfleet Electric Tramways Ltd. The four routes in operation by December 1903 were not very successful, largely because the company did not generate its own electricity. BET made an attempt to economise in 1908 by merging the management with that of its Sheerness & District

Map key: —— BUSES ········ TRAMS

the driver frantically swings the starting handle afresh. "That's right driver, wind it right up. I knew you hadn't wound it enough at Gravesend to go the whole way." ' The issues ceased in December 1931, but Shipp had paved the way for the later M&D journal *Inside Only* which started 16 years later, by which time he was District Superintendent at Gillingham.

The company acquired the first of its subsidiary operations on 1 March 1929 when BET decided to close the tramway at Gravesend and Northfleet and replace it with a fleet of 16 lowbridge Leyland Titan buses.

Maidstone & District's 'northwest corner' was far from secure, however. Herbert Morrison's London Passenger Transport Bill, 'changed by the Conservatives until he no longer supported it' (according to John Hibbs in his 1969 *History of British Bus Services*), became law in 1933. The Act set up the London Passenger Transport Board and permitted it to absorb undertakings in the wider 'London Country' area. M&D was obliged to give up its Dartford and Northfleet depots and the routes associated with them, including those from Gravesend purchased for £2,000 in December 1926 from Josiah Roberts' and Roger Old's 'Co-operated Bus Service'. M&D was also required to hand over 10 single-deck buses, 11 coaches and 34 Leyland Titan TD1 double-deckers. For its overall losses it received £76,964 4s 2d in compensation — but retained its Overcliffe garage in Gravesend, together with restricted operating rights in that borough.

Electrical Power & Traction Co Ltd. In 1913, however, it decided to adopt motorbuses. A subsidiary company, North Kent Motor Services, was established at the Dover Road, Northfleet, tramways depot. Whereas the trams were maroon and cream, the buses ran in BET's Brunswick green and broken white, so when M&D outstationed a pair of vehicles at the same depot they looked very much at home. This was very much in line with BET policy, which always encouraged a degree of in-house rivalry, and for a few years the two firms ran the Chatham–Gravesend route jointly. NKMS route 'A', meanwhile, had thwarted a Balfour Beatty group's plan to link the Dartford tramway with Swanscombe.

Maidstone & District took over the NKMS operation in 1920, and the Dover Road shed became its Northfleet depot. From here M&D set out to consolidate its position at Gravesend and establish itself in the Dartford area. In 1921 it built offices and a 33-vehicle garage at Overcliffe, Gravesend, but it was not until 1926 that the construction of a 20-vehicle garage in Priory Road, Dartford, was commenced. A lasting memorial for this depot proved to be the two volumes of an M&D house magazine called *The Green 'Un*, devised and edited by E. M. C. Shipp at Priory Road, to bring together news and views of the whole company. Its tone was set in the very first (March 1930) issue: '[A] dear old lady sitting on the front bench seat watches the driver start the bus with one swing of the handle. Halfway to Swanscombe the bus breaks down and

The Medway Towns

From 1913 to February 1916, M&D outstationed three vehicles in rented accommodation owned by the Strood Motor & Engineering Co Ltd. It then acquired land in Fox Street, Gillingham, as a temporary base — and that in turn was given up in 1921 with the opening of a garage, initially for 26 vehicles, in Nelson Road. The yard was shared for a couple of years with Andrew's Dairy and all its attendant milk churns and horse-drawn floats.

The original Nelson Road fleet consisted largely of Tilling-Stevens TS3A saloons and double-decker buses, plus several Leyland N charabancs for private hires and local excursions and

Until the addition to the Leyland range of the lengthened O-model charabanc in 1922, only one-day excursions had been undertaken by M&D. This bigger model, again bodied by Harrington, makes an interesting contrast with the earlier N-type charabanc with separate doors to each row of seats. Instead, this vehicle has just two doors and a central gangway — and, strictly speaking, is not a true charabanc. Three- to 10-day trips were now on offer.
Alan Lambert collection

The trams of the Gravesend & Northfleet Electric Tramways Ltd were replaced in March 1929 by new Leyland TD1 Titan double-deckers in a dark red and ivory livery, with the BET logo on their flanks. M&D assigned £43,620 to the G&NET for the purchase of the vehicles and then operated them on its behalf. No 299 (KP 3392) passes over the redundant tramlines *en route* to the 'Leather Bottel'. The 16 Titans concerned passed into the M&D fleet proper in January 1930.
Colin Morris collection

21

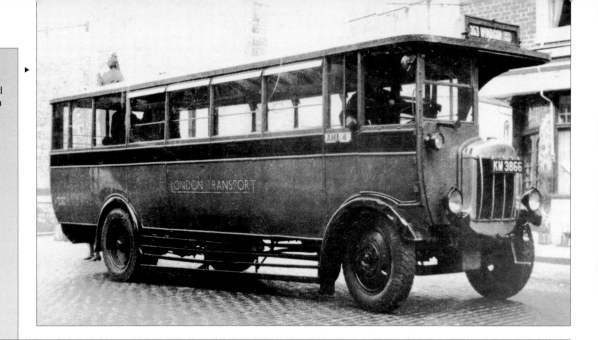

When the London Passenger Transport Board was set up in 1933, Maidstone & District lost its services based upon Dartford and Northfleet and was required to surrender 55 vehicles to London Transport. M&D Tilling-Stevens B9A saloon No 405 (KM 3866) of 1926 was one of these. At first, its new owners gave it 'GENERAL' fleetnames, but LT's Amersham depot had updated that by the winter of 1933/4, when it was photographed passing Windsor Castle. *Colin Morris collection*

KT 1912, originally delivered as a Tilling-Stevens TS with a Tilling single-deck body, is a good representative of that hard-working type of chassis. It was new in 1914, received a similar body from a sister vehicle in 1924, became No 4 in a fleet-numbering system introduced in 1925 and that year was rebuilt from normal- to forward-control TS6 specification by Tilling-Stevens, receiving this new 51-seat body by Short of Rochester. It then gained pneumatic tyres, and served until 1930. *Alan Lambert collection*

No 307 (KM 3876) was delivered in August 1926 specifically to 'chase' the vehicles run by small rival firms. It was a Guy 30cwt with 14-seat bodywork by Short. Whereas five sister vehicles by the same coachbuilder were wooden-framed, No 307 was Short Bros' first all-metal vehicle, built to Maidstone & District design. There was much 'chasing' to be done in the Medway Towns, and this chirpy little bus spent some four years largely in that role. *Alan Lambert collection*

At the Nelson Road, Gillingham, depot in June 1924, driver Albert Gale and conductor Sidney Wainwright pose with KT 3070, a 1914-vintage Tilling-Stevens TS3 with open-top Dodson bodywork. M&D route A had become service 1 when letters were abandoned in 1920. Wainwright served M&D for 45 years, rising to the rank of inspector. Upon retirement he founded a highly successful social club for retired M&D personnel at Gillingham. *Colin Morris collection*

23

The vehicles, property, goodwill and licences of Orange Coaches (Chatham) were bought by M&D on 5 March 1931 for £20,000. By that time, Alfred 'Jack' Kelcey was in partnership with William Murrell and Alec Hammond. The fleet acquired by M&D comprised 14 Gilfords and one Thornycroft, the oldest being a 1926 Gilford LL15 20-seater, KM 8049. This was allotted M&D fleetnumber 722 but was one of three not operated.
Alfred Kelcey collection

When the MDBOA members sold their vehicles to M&D, 26 single-deck buses were involved, including those built by Commer, Morris, Chevrolet, Graham, Dennis, Thornycroft, Bean, Reo, Star and Federal. M&D paid a total of £21,400 for the businesses concerned. No more than five are believed to have operated with M&D, although only this smart Commer Invader 6TK with 20-seat Chatham Motor Co bodywork (ex-Langton) received a fleetnumber (809) and M&D livery.
Omnibus Society

tours. In 1926 the depot was provided with some Guy 14-seaters to chase the local opposition — and that there was aplenty. Among several ex-servicemen who spent their postwar gratuities upon the purchase of small buses was Lt Col J. H. Langton of Gillingham, with his red and blue 'Ubique' identity — the colours and motto respectively of the Royal Engineers. A Maltese, Vincent Vella, chose the girl's name 'Theresie' from that island for his operation based in Medway Street, Chatham, and built up a fleet of 13 vehicles — mostly Reo saloons — in a brown and ginger livery. Theresie Safety Coaches Ltd was the first Medway operator to come under the control of M&D, reaching an accommodation whereby the latter initially controlled the shares of Vella's company and then purchased outright the goodwill and 10 Reo saloons for £6,273 on 31 March 1930. Prior to that, M&D had bought the goodwill and licences only of William Larkin's Wouldham service for £200.

Meanwhile Tom Goddard and Alfred 'Jack' Kelcey formed 'Orange Coaches' at Gillingham, basing the vehicles at a garage in Granville Road. Although they ran a stage-carriage service,

Chatham–Gillingham–Upper Gillingham, most of their vehicles were employed upon express workings: Rainham (Kent)–Gillingham–London and Gravesend–Gillingham–Sheerness. The local service was numbered 60 — 'because you've got the other 59 and most of them are chasing after us', George French told.

Neither Vella nor Goddard & Kelcey became involved with an exercise in mutual support engaged in by most other small operators in Medway during the later 'Twenties. This was the Medway District Bus Owners' Association, formed to protect each member from the possibility of licence-refusals from any of the three Medway councils. It published its first joint timetable in 1929, as two further threats to the members' future loomed.

First was the Parliamentary plan to regulate the bus industry, which was to be included in the Road Traffic Act 1930. Second was the news that Maidstone & District, which had gained a controlling interest in the Chatham & District Light Railways, was about to replace the tram services with 'a sufficient number of buses'. Humphrey Robinson was elected Chairman of the company, two-thirds of which was owned by M&D.

▲ Maidstone & District gained financial control of Chatham & District
Light Railways and replaced the trams with the motorbuses of the
Chatham & District Traction Co. M&D purchased a fleet of Leyland
TD1 Titans, and its subsidiary paid the parent company under a hire-
purchase agreement. George French placed the order with Leyland
on condition that 'the whole 30 [be] put into operation on the same
date as the complete disbandment of the local tramway services'.
Colin Morris collection

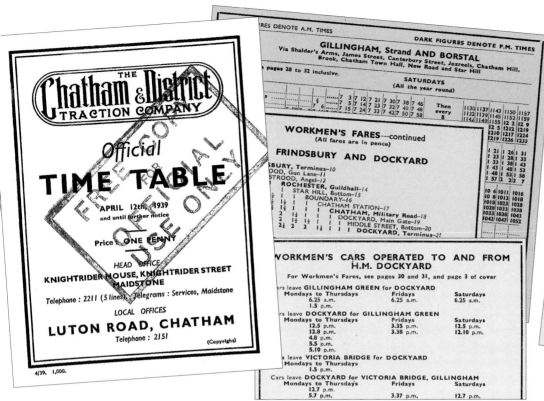

THE Chatham & District TRACTION COMPANY

Official

TIME TABLE

APRIL 12th, 1939
and until further notice

Price ONE PENNY

HEAD OFFICE
KNIGHTRIDER HOUSE, KNIGHTRIDER STREET
MAIDSTONE

Telephone : 2211 (5 lines) · Telegrams : Services, Maidstone

LOCAL OFFICES

LUTON ROAD, CHATHAM
Telephone : 2151

(Copyright)

4/39. 1,000.

LIGHT FIGURES DENOTE A.M. TIMES   DARK FIGURES DENOTE P.M. TIMES

GILLINGHAM, Strand AND BORSTAL
Via Shalder's Arms, James Street, Canterbury Street, Jezreels, Chatham Hill,
Brook, Chatham Town Hall, New Road and Star Hill.

... pages 28 to 32 inclusive.

SATURDAYS
(All the year round)

WORKMEN'S FARES—continued
(All fares are in pence)

FRINDSBURY AND DOCKYARD

...SBURY, Terminus—10
...OOD, Gun Lane—11
...TROOD, Angel—12
ROCHESTER, Guildhall—14
STAR HILL, Bottom—15
BOUNDARY—16
CHATHAM STATION—17
CHATHAM, Military Road—18
DOCKYARD, Main Gate—19
MIDDLE STREET, Bottom—20
DOCKYARD, Terminus—21

WORKMEN'S CARS OPERATED TO AND FROM H.M. DOCKYARD

For Workmen's Fares, see pages 30 and 31, and page 3 of cover

Cars leave GILLINGHAM GREEN for DOCKYARD

Mondays to Thursdays	Fridays	Saturdays
6.25 a.m.	6.25 a.m.	6.25 a.m.
1.5 p.m.		

Cars leave DOCKYARD for GILLINGHAM GREEN

Mondays to Thursdays	Fridays	Saturdays
12.5 p.m.	3.35 p.m.	12.5 p.m.
12.8 p.m.	3.38 p.m.	12.10 p.m.
4.8 p.m.		
5.5 p.m.		
5.10 p.m.		

Cars leave VICTORIA BRIDGE for DOCKYARD

Mondays to Thursdays
1.5 p.m.

Cars leave DOCKYARD for VICTORIA BRIDGE, GILLINGHAM

Mondays to Thursdays	Fridays	Saturdays
12.7 p.m.		12.7 p.m.
5.7 p.m.	3.37 p.m.	

13809

THE Maidstone & District MOTOR SERVICES LTD

EMPLOYEE'S LEAVING REPORT

Date of Leaving 18ᵗʰ SEPTEMBER 1939

Name M. RIDGE

Depot at which Employed GILLINGHAM

Trade CONDUCTOR

Cause of Leaving

OWN ACCORD
(ENLISTED)

Reported by

Confirmed

This Copy to be sent to Employees' Records Department
(Head Office)

The latter ordered an initial 30 Leyland Titan double-deckers to be delivered by 30 September 1930, the last day of the trams. And, indeed, they were. But a best-kept secret has been discovered in the Leyland General Manager's report to his Board of Directors in February 1931: he referred to an 'unaccountable wholesale failure of frames [at a point immediately behind the front spring rear-end bracket] on vehicles supplied to the Chatham & District . . . At the time of dictating this note no less than 14 frames have failed, all at the same point in the nearside member, and arrangements have been made to replace the whole fleet by frames of a thicker section.' The matter was referred to the frame suppliers amid confusion as to whether a fault in the material or the 'heavily-cambered' roads of Chatham was responsible. This may explain the loan to C&D of some

Maidstone & District Tilling-Stevens double-deckers during that period. An additional 13 TD1 Titans, in the C&D colours of pea green, ivory and ginger, were delivered by September 1931. Clearly the problem had been worked out, but the Titans were replaced by Bristol GO5G (briefly) and K5G double-deckers just before World War 2.

Gillingham depot was enlarged in 1928, eventually becoming M&D's biggest, with more than 600 staff. Several M&D drivers transferred to the C&D depot at Luton (Chatham), to join the 'converted' tram drivers stationed there. M&D's expansion based upon Gillingham involved the purchase of Hucks Bros' business and service from Burham to Chatham for £3,850 and Fred Sands' Hoo–Chatham and Gillingham–Stoke routes for £1,400 in January and February 1933.

▲ The acquisition of Sheppey Motor Transport in January 1930,
followed by the purchase of Enterprise Motor Services the following
December, gave Maidstone & District a right also to the established
express service from Sheerness to London, which M&D identified as
its service E6. A later variation went from Sheerness to Walthamstow.
At Leyton in June 1937 is 1931 Leyland Tiger TS2 No 646 (KR 7411),
a 31-seat Harrington-bodied express coach. *S. L. Poole / LBPG*

Sheerness

For administrative purposes, M&D decided in the 'Thirties to include Faversham and Sittingbourne depots in its designated Sheerness District. The premises at Preston Street, Faversham, had been made into a proper depot in 1920 and, over the next decade, were extended to accommodate 15 vehicles. Services to Newnham and Doddington were added in 1922, to Lenham in 1929 and later to Grafty Green. By 1930 some 60 staff were divided between the depot and a booking office in nearby Court Street.

Largely because of an unsuitable bridge over The Swale at Kingsferry, and yet another early BET presence, M&D was comparatively late gaining access in its own right to the Isle of Sheppey. BET's interest on the island started in 1900 when it launched a local company and provided funds for an electricity-generating station in Sheerness. It also planned a tramway system, but could not get permission to cross the local railway company's lines. Thus, when it opened in April 1903, the trams could not reach Queenborough and were confined to some 2½ miles of track centred on Sheerness Clock Tower. The 'Sheerness & District' was therefore extremely vulnerable to opposition; it began to suffer such in December 1913 in the form of two open-topped Dennis double-deckers run by T. Standen & Sons of Shortlands Road, Sittingbourne. Standen set up an office in Sheerness East, engaged in a fares war with the trams and introduced a route to Eastchurch with Dennis saloons.

When Maidstone & District vehicles were sent to the Isle of Sheppey in January 1930 to supplement or replace those taken over from Sheppey Motor Transport, they tended to be somewhat elderly saloon buses. Single-deck buses were the norm because of a low railway bridge on the single access road. The interior of KK 8862, a Leyland SG7 with 37-seat Beadle bodywork, gives an idea of the period. Since this vehicle was not withdrawn until 1931, it just might have been one of them.
Alan Lambert collection

BET then sent Daimler saloons and a charabanc to work for Sheerness & District, and it seems that M&D provided maintenance facilities and drivers for them. The BET buses ran between Sheerness and Queenborough and, in conjunction with M&D, between Chatham and Sittingbourne — Standen's home base. Trapped as it was in northwest Sheppey, the tram system ground to a halt in June 1917 — the first in Britain to be put out of business by motorbuses. The Sheerness & District Power & Traction Co came to an agreement with Standen soon after, and the two pooled their resources as the Sheppey Motor Transport Co Ltd, with some seven vehicles. Standen bought out the BET interest in April 1919, but BET continued to supply dark green Daimler buses for its use until 1925. From June 1923 Thomas Standen Jnr ran an all-Dennis private-hire fleet in a blue livery at Sittingbourne, the combined Standen and SMT fleets rising to 31 buses over the next decade.

From February 1926 Standen's Sheppey Motor Transport Co was itself confronted by a competitor. Robert Grimer placed two Dennis saloons in service at Queenborough and built up his 'Enterprise Motor Services' until he was deploying a fleet of 17 buses and coaches — the latter competing also on an express route between Sheerness and London. From 1928 M&D again took an active interest on Sheppey, when it made an operational agreement with Enterprise which led to an eventual takeover. The 'right battle-royal', as driver George 'Huckleberry' Finn described it, came to an end on 7 January 1930, when the goodwill and 22 vehicles of SMT and Standen's of Sittingbourne were jointly purchased by M&D for £30,000. Several key members of staff came to M&D from SMT, notably Engineer-in-Charge Sam Pettican, who became M&D's first Sheerness District Superintendent.

Maidstone & District achieved a clean sweep on Sheppey when Enterprise and 12 buses were transferred into its ownership on 17 December 1930 for £18,500. When Pettican moved on to Gillingham depot in 1932, 'Uncle Bob' Grimer replaced him as District Superintendent, Sheerness, until his retirement in 1952.

There were no enclosed-top double-deckers in the depot at this time, although some were later brought to the island in two pieces, the top deck being replaced after negotiating the low railway bridge at Kingsferry. The buses continued to terminate at The Broadway, Sheerness, but an improvement in passenger facilities was created in 1932 with a new coach station at the west end of the High Street.

With Standen's restricted to its original goods-haulage work, M&D fitted out a depot for 22 vehicles at East Street, Sittingbourne, in 1931. On 4 September of that year M&D reinforced its hold when Sittingbourne & District Motors Ltd — known also as the Sittingbourne–Milton Motor Service — sold the goodwill of its Rodmersham Green service for £450. The route became part of M&D's service 43.

Hastings and Bexhill

In 1919 M&D opened a garage for four buses at Earl Street, Hastings, in what used to be a banana warehouse. Although Rye had been designated as part of the M&D area, it was not until June 1922 that the company arrived in that delightful town and outstationed a vehicle intermittently to work its service to Hastings. Then, in 1923, came a short-lived service worked by Hawkhurst depot, to Northiam and Hastings, and, as M&D began to move into a proposed Southdown enclave, a Hastings circular taking in Battle and Bexhill started in May 1924. The company's claim strengthened that year with a service to Little Common and Cooden.

BEXHILL, SIDLEY & NINFIELD BUS.

Additions came slowly in Hastings and Bexhill because the towns had been joined and served by the trams of the Hastings Tramways Co, which started in 1905. Although not a subsidiary of BET or another large tramway group, HTC nevertheless established its own generating station at Ore in northeast Hastings. A main depot for the trams was built in Silverhill and a subsidiary one at Bulverhythe. From 1919 M&D began running along the tram routes to reach destinations farther afield and was required by Hastings Corporation to charge a minimum fare of 3d (1.25p) whilst doing so.

At Bexhill, M&D encountered a small rival called 'Bexhill & District Motor Bus Services' with its garage and yard at Little Common. It was originally equipped with small Ford Model T saloons. In October 1923 the first of three Vulcans was introduced by proprietors Reg Carter and George Lidstone, and Jack Baker, later a long-serving employee of M&D, joined the firm: 'When you stood on the rear platform of the Fords, you could look right over the roof.' A Morris 14-seater completed the fleet, the colours of which were black on white.

After much chasing, M&D bought the business of Carter & Lidstone for £6,550 on 19 July 1926. The first M&D vehicle to

BEXHILL—NINFIELD SERVICE.

From I.B. and S.C. Railway to Sidley, via Amherst Road, Lunsford Cross and Ninfield, and vice versa.

Leave L.B. & S.C.	Leave Ninfield.
*8.0	*8.30
*9.15	*10.0
*9.45 B	*11.25 B
11.0	12.0
12.0 B	1.45 B
12.30	3.30 B
2.0 B	4.30
3.0 B	5.0 B
4.0	6.30
5.0 B	7.0 B
6.0	7.45
7.0	9.15 B
7.30B	9.15
8.45	

* Not Sundays.   B Battle Bus.

FARES.

L.B.S.C.Rly. to		Ninfield Post Office to	
The Mill	3d	Pashley	2d
St. Mary's Cottages	4d	The Thorne	3d
Freezeland Lane	4d	Lunsford Cross	3d
Lunsford Cross	4d	Freezeland Lane	4d
The Thorne	5d	St. Mary's Cottages	5d
Pashley	5d	The Mill	5d
Ninfield Lower Street	6d	Sidley	6d
Ninfield Post Office	8d	L.B.S.C.Rly	8d

It does not matter where you are

IF YOU WANT A CAR

RING UP COODEN 8

For the QUICKEST & CHEAPEST place to Hire a Car.

EIGHTPENCE PER MILE

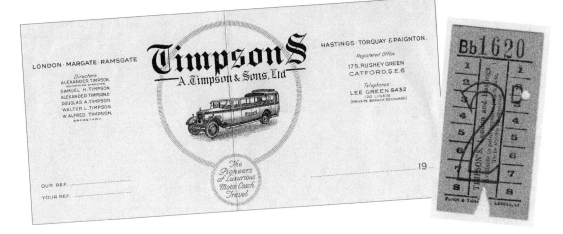

The most modern of the 66 vehicles acquired from A. Timpson & Sons Ltd at Hastings in March 1934 were six AEC Regent 661 double-deckers with 56-seat bodywork by Harrington of Hove, Sussex. DY 7858, in the cream and chocolate livery of that Catford-based firm, was repainted in M&D dark green and broken white and given the fleetnumber 107. All six continued to serve locally, but were rebodied in 1942. *Alan Townsin collection*

arrive at the Church Hill, Little Common, depot — utilised by M&D for one year — was a Leyland N charabanc. M&D then removed to a new garage in Terminus Road, Bexhill, with space for 18 vehicles.

Hastings Corporation, anxious to undertake road improvements, pleaded in vain for HTC to run motorbuses instead of trams, and showed an impulsive generosity to anyone else who was willing to run them. At one stage M&D asked for 15 new licences — and was astonished to be granted 30. The Corporation's munificence was extended also to A. Timpson & Sons Ltd of London, which had intended to run only an express service from Hastings to the capital. In addition it was awarded stage-carriage licences and opened offices at 15 Castle Street and 56 Robertson Street — and a garage in Brook Street beside another occupied by M&D since 1920. Timpson's established 17 route variations around the borough, its cream and chocolate livery appearing upon Leyland Lion, ADC 426 and AEC Regal saloons by 1933. That year Hickman Bros (Skinner's) sold its stage-carriage services to Timpson's, together with 10 of its vehicles. Timpson's celebrated by buying six AEC Regent double-deckers. Acquiring Timpson's Hastings operations, premises and 66 vehicles, on 19 March 1934, cost M&D £106,488 — its most expensive purchase of a rival.

Meanwhile, HTC set out to replace its 65 trams with Guy six-wheeled trolleybuses — eight open-top double-deckers and 50 centre-exit single-deckers — and on 1 April 1928 an inaugural run was made between Hollington and the Fishmarket. The trolleybuses became popular with tourists and local people alike, but trouble with the generating station proved extremely costly.

In October 1935 M&D, unable to purchase HTC because of the latter's statutory status, made a 'total investment' in its assets and activities, for the sum of £101,833. Hastings Tramways Co — a name it retained, despite its trolleybus fleet — thus became a subsidiary of M&D, whose directors replaced those of HTC upon the board, and all its staff were kept on. The trolleybuses were repainted from their maroon and ivory livery into BET dark green and broken white, and route numbers encircled with a ring M&D-fashion, but the fleetname 'Hastings & District' was displayed.

The generating station was closed, and electricity supplied by Hastings and by Bexhill was used for traction instead. Both Hastings Corporation and M&D would have preferred to substitute the original trolleybuses with motorbuses, but the onset of World War 2 and its attendant restrictions put off that day, and the company was obliged to commence that replacement programme in 1940 with 20 AEC 661T 54-seat double-deck trolleybuses.

From 1926, staff at M&D's Brook Street premises had administrative responsibility for the 14-vehicle garage at Lower Lake, Battle, and, from 1927 to 1936, two buses outstationed at Herstmonceux. The acquisition of Timpson's premises in Brook Street, the 'No 2 shed', brought the capacity up to 68 buses. Officially M&D's property from 11 November 1935, the Silverhill garage at Beaufort Road, St Leonards, and its satellite in Bexhill Road remained concerned solely with trolleybuses at that time.

▲ In 1928 Hastings Tramways Co prolonged the life of its generating station at Ore and much of its overhead equipment in the streets by resisting Hastings Corporation's pleas for the trams to be replaced by motorbuses. Instead, trolleybuses were substituted, all of Guy manufacture. DY 4969 was one of eight open-top BTX-type double-deckers with 57-seat Dodson bodywork. The fleetname was 'Hastings & District'. *Colin Morris collection*

▲ Typical of the Tilling-Stevens single-deck buses working for Maidstone & District in the 'Thirties, including the Hastings area, was No 519 (KP 3047), a B10A2 31-seater with observation-style rear windows at the rear three-quarter position. The vehicle was bodied by Short at its Rochester factory — a line of business set up after World War 1 to keep its workforce intact after the need for military seaplanes declined somewhat. *Richard Rosa collection*

In M&D's dark green and broken white livery, replacement trolleybus No 1 (BDY 776), the first of an eventual 45 double-deckers delivered by 1948, stands at Beaufort Road, Silverhill, in June 1940. One of 20 English Electric-bodied AEC 661T models, it sports 'Hastings Tramway Company' fleetnames. Behind it is 1928 Guy single-decker No 28 with RSJ bodywork. In the background, one of M&D's six Leyland Titan TD5 open-toppers of 1939 departs on service 30 for Rye. *Alan Townsin collection* ▲

Tunbridge Wells

Although the 1914 agreement with East Surrey decreed that M&D should go no farther west than Tunbridge Wells, the founding of a company there in 1909 had already set in train events which would lead to such a line being breached in 1935. Col John Egginton and his nephew Raymond Marshall raised the money for the Autocar Co Ltd, with its registered office in the Opera House Buildings, and appointed Oscar Pritchard as General Manager. Pritchard became Managing Director of the revamped Autocar (Tunbridge Wells) Co Ltd in 1910 as a result of his success with three All British Car Co (ABC) double-deckers. The operator became a public limited company on 12 November 1913 and took the name Autocar Services Ltd. When A. G. Ingerfield joined it that year, only one ABC was still active, and that had been converted to a charabanc: 'Andy Maxwell used to drive it in his trilby hat.'

Leylands were much liked at Autocar and were used to establish routes to Borough Green, Hadlow, Cranbrook, Hawkhurst, Edenbridge, Uckfield and other destinations radiating from

Tunbridge Wells and Tonbridge. Soon after a service to Sevenoaks was started in 1919, this was extended to Farnborough (Kent), but 18 months later it was taken over by East Surrey. Arthur J. Hawkins (founder of the latter), Oscar Pritchard and George French became great friends, visiting each other regularly and creating an easy-going atmosphere on M&D's western flank.

In February 1923 Autocar was faced with a serious rival. The brothers Thomas and James B. Elliott formed Redcar Services Ltd at Tunbridge Wells and set out to match Pritchard route for route. A price war started which brought the fare between Tunbridge Wells and Tonbridge down to a penny; Redcar succeeded in getting Autocar fined 5s (25p) for operating a bus ⁄₁₀in over the legal width, such was the level of animosity between them. The scenario changed somewhat in 1928. A takeover of Autocar by East Surrey had been mooted since 1923, but old friends got together: Maidstone & District took a financial interest in Redcar. Using East Surrey as its agent, the London General Omnibus Co Ltd acquired just over half of Autocar's

shares and cleared debts run up in the fight with Redcar. Despite that, Autocar became effectively a subsidiary of East Surrey, with that firm's Albert Makovski on the board. Oscar Pritchard retired from the industry in 1929.

Maidstone & District's involvement with Redcar included the joint purchase of five Leyland Tigers and four Titans in 1930/1, for use by the latter in its own livery. French and Hawkins set up a proper co-ordination of routes and fares on Autocar and Redcar services — the former adopting Redcar's route numbers — pending the outcome of negotiations which turned East Surrey into London General Country Services and led to the establishment, in 1933, of the London Passenger Transport Board. Since most of Autocar's services were outside the area allotted to the LPTB, M&D was able to acquire the entire share capital of Autocar

Services Ltd, which, for a two-year period, it ran in the mauve and ivory livery with 'Autocar' fleetname.

The assets of Redcar were finally purchased by M&D on 19 February 1935 for £101,192. Included were 54 vehicles and the Redcar garages at Avebury Avenue, Tonbridge, and Upper Grosvenor Road, Tunbridge Wells. Autocar formally joined the fold on 1 May 1935, when the majority of its services, the St John's Road garage and 43 buses were purchased for £91,688.

From 1927, in the midst of the Tunbridge Wells 'bus wars', Victor Avard had developed a series of routes from that town to Hawkenbury, Horsmonden, Parsons Green, Pembury and elsewhere. The services and 13 vehicles, in a buff livery, of the Tunbridge Wells Victor Motor Transport Co Ltd were bought by M&D for £17,000 on 9 April 1935. Three Chevrolets and three Bedfords joined the M&D fleet and acquired numbers.

Maidstone and Central Administration

Humphrey Robinson returned from World War 1 with the rank of Major, and M&D promptly brought in a long-lasting system of ranks for its drivers — leading driver, assistant foreman and foreman driver.

The Upper Stone Street premises gained increased office accommodation in 1920, the year that the share capital was raised to £150,000. On 29 April 1921 the Thomas Tilling organisation took a financial interest and its Walter Wolsey joined the board; 1922 marked a great leap forward — new capital was raised by going public, and the first bus station in England was built at the corner of Palace Avenue. Maintenance facilities were provided at a new Central Repair Works in Postley Road, said at the time to be the most up-to-

In 1922 Maidstone & District built the first proper bus station in England on a site in Palace Avenue leased to the company by Maidstone Corporation. KE 9664, a Guy J 25cwt charabanc with 14-seat bodywork by Beadle, has been pressed into stage-carriage service on route 29 to Burham. In the background, Leyland and Tilling-Stevens service buses take on passengers, while a young company porter checks the address on a parcel. *M&D and East Kent Bus Club*

date in the country. All sections were contained within their own walls beneath the one roof-span.

During the next financial year, however, a trade union dispute reduced M&D's operating profits to World War 1 level. The Lloyd George coalition Government had encouraged wage cuts for miners and, in 1919, for railway workers. The railwaymen successfully nipped that in the bud. Then came the turn of road transport. Early in 1923 M&D announced a wage reduction of one penny per hour for drivers but not for conductors. Both were called out on strike in May 1923 by the Transport & General Workers' Union. Maidstone and Gillingham were affected on the first day, and the rest of the depots joined in. Vehicles owned by the Co-operative Transport Society (the 'Co-operabancs') were sent from Folkestone and, crewed by strikers, ran for a couple of months, but gave up because no fitters had joined the strike. The unrest petered out in October and ended in defeat for the crewmen, some of whom were reinstated at reduced rates. Within a few years, however, the wages of drivers had overtaken those of fitters — some, like 'Freddie' Fridd, laying down their tools to take a job behind the wheel. The company had learned much which stood it in good stead for confronting the General Strike in 1926.

Whilst Robinson was a shy man whom the workforce hardly ever saw, George French wanted to be involved in everything. At Postley Works, French designed bus and coach bodies, machine parts, improved working spaces, even complete bus stations and depots. Working for George French was a turbulent experience for everyone concerned. First, he considered all members of staff part of his extended family, and treated them accordingly. There were few who, at one time or another, were not 'sacked', only to be reinstated almost immediately and even given a pay rise. His young cousin Walter J. Flexman was 'sacked' along with everyone else, but was nevertheless sent on his way in 1923 with a Commer lorry as a gift to help set up a business in Bognor Regis. Yet a common sense of purpose prevailed; the consensus of opinion was an affectionate 'you knew where you were with George French' — praise indeed! The death of his father resulted in George's being raised to the status of Director in January 1926, but that didn't diminish his 'hands-on' approach one iota.

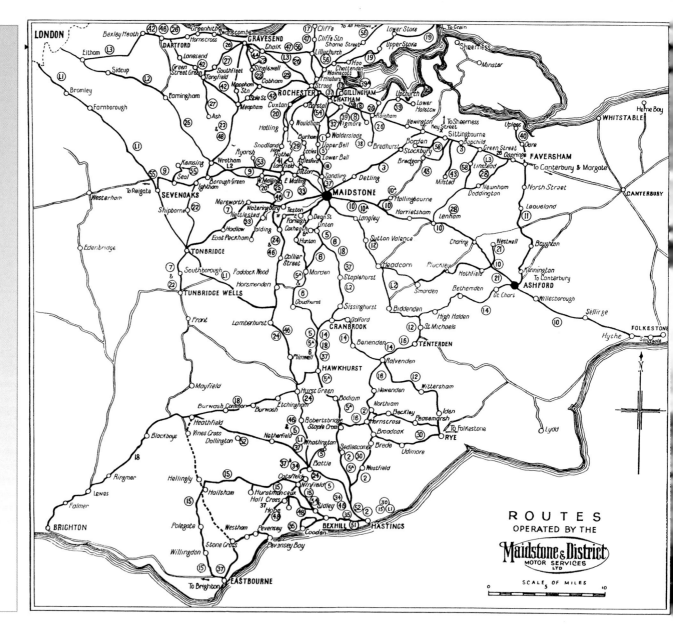

Maidstone & District's network of stage-carriage services in the spring of 1929, some nine months before the company made Sheerness and the Isle of Sheppey part of its territory. The extent of the infilling to the west of Hastings, in an area originally allotted to Southdown, is considerable. The company's express services to London are indicated in an 'L' series for 'London', rather than the later 'E'.
Colin Morris collection

ROUTES
OPERATED BY THE

Maidstone & District
MOTOR SERVICES LTD

SCALE OF MILES

INDEX

The Company reserves the right to alter any of the Services without previous notice.

By 1925 the fleet size had risen to 140 vehicles, of which just over a quarter were double-deckers. The following year, the Palace Avenue bus station was extended into Lower Stone Street, turning it from one of the quietest into one of the busiest thoroughfares in town. In 1927 M&D moved into a garage for 11 vehicles in Station Road, Ashford — an increasingly important outpost for both M&D and East Kent. At Tenterden, R. & J. Bennett Ltd provided a parcels and booking office and continued to lease its yard at West Cross as an outstation for M&D until it opened its own garage in the High Street in 1927. Bennett's was eventually purchased, on 28 May 1935, for £1,000, this including two vehicles; one of these, a Commer Centaur, served for a further 12 years with M&D. The company also took possession of the architecturally charming 'Tudor Rose', a 15th-century Tudor hall, which became its local public face in Tenterden.

Borough Green garage came into operation in 1927 — then little more than a four-bus shed for overnight accommodation. From that beginning it was developed into one of the more important smaller rural depots. At this time there were also outstations at East Peckham, Horsmonden, Eccles, Hawkhurst and Northiam, plus one at Charing which closed in 1927.

In 1928 Tilling and BET interests in territorial companies were formalised by the founding of the Tilling & British Automobile Traction Co Ltd. It was Tilling & BAT which negotiated a deal with the four British main-line railway companies, which thereafter decided not to run their own bus services. Instead, for instance, under the provisions of the Southern Railway (Road Transport) Act 1928, that company opted to buy itself a part of the existing bus industry in its operating area. The Southern Railway paid 48s 6d (£2.42½) each for its M&D shares as against £3.25 for Southdown's, £2.25 for Hants & Dorset's and £1.32½ for Aldershot & District's, and Lt Col Gilbert Szlumper and Ralph Davidson, respectively Assistant General Manager and Chief Accountant of the SR, joined the M&D board on 10 February 1930. This infusion contributed strongly to the raising of the M&D share capital to £700,000 on 5 July 1934.

As a direct result of the planning for and implementation of the Road Traffic Act 1930, some 19 rival undertakings sold their businesses to M&D between April 1929 and October 1933. The first and last of those represent the two largest acquisitions in the Maidstone vicinity — Red Road Cars of Knightrider Street, Maidstone, and Lenham, with eight small vehicles, for £2,750, and the Weald of Kent Transport Co, with 18 saloon buses and

coaches, for £19,476. The latter was an important addition to the company's stage-carriage network around Tenterden and The Weald and to its coaching activity also.

Both garage and office accommodation at Upper Stone Street had become inadequate by 1928, so M&D purchased Knightrider House in Maidstone, and this became the new registered office of the company. Behind this was built a large garage, which, after extensions in 1936, provided room for 86 vehicles.

The company's financial health progressed apace, and the yearly net profit passed the £100,000 mark for the first time in 1936. On 11 August that year the share capital was raised to £1 million — Tilling & BAT and the Southern Railway holding 85,371 shares apiece, and the remainder in the hands of other companies and private individuals.

There was a marked shift in vehicle policy after 1929. Although second-hand examples continued to enter the fleet, M&D took

delivery of its last new Tilling-Stevens that year, and Leyland buses gained the ascendancy. Yet several other makes which found their way into the fleet during the 'Thirties led to further purchases. Thus new Gilford coaches, Morris-Commercial saloons, AEC double-deckers, AEC Regal saloons, Dennis Ace saloons and Bristol double-deckers were bought direct from the manufacturers, the larger saloons and double-deckers fitted with oil engines. By the outbreak of World War 2 in 1939, over 200 of M&D's fleet of 560 buses were fitted with this type of power unit. Nevertheless, the large number of petrol-engined vehicles acquired from smaller operators in the 'Thirties tended to delay the switch to diesel bunkerage at the company's depots.

On 7 August 1935 Percy Graefe, the Secretary and now Commercial Manager, presided at a dinner and concert to celebrate George French's 25 years at Maidstone. A magnificent grandfather clock was presented to him and his wife Minnie, which

DESCRIPTIVE GUIDE
TO THE
OMNIBUS SERVICES
OPERATED BY,
The Maidstone & District
MOTOR SERVICES
LTD.

PRICE 2D.

In 1929 M&D issued an attractive 112-page illustrated guide to its system at a time when 'the fleet consists of 400 cars'. Included were the London services, special trips, combined boat and bus tickets and similar 'bus and dance' tickets to entertainment halls. It continued the notion that the company was 'inaugurated as long ago as 1908'. The Tilling-Stevens saloon depicted upon the cover seems to be displaying a large amount of Tilling green. *Roger Davies collection*

▲ On 1 November 1933 M&D purchased the goodwill, services and 19 vehicles of The Weald of Kent Transport Co, Tenterden. The firm had been started in 1925 by C. E. E. Palin, who was joined by C. H. J. Nevell and Thomas 'Jock' Cousin in 1928, and was an important addition also to M&D's coaching activity. This Strachans-bodied Thornycroft Cygnet CD/AC6, No 851 (KJ 8117) of 1932, was photographed whilst under repair at the chassis manufacturer's Basingstoke works in April 1934. *Colin Morris collection*

◄ George Flexman French at his (dark) green-topped desk in Knightrider House, Maidstone, registered office of Maidstone & District from its purchase in 1928. During the 1790s, the house had been the rented abode of William Shipley, founder of the Royal Society of Arts, and it bore a plaque to that effect during the company's occupation. It was also the birthplace of Roy Plomley, who devised and for many years presented the BBC's *Desert Island Discs. Colin Morris collection*

Marked up for a visit to Leeds village, home of the famous moated castle, is a very unusual Leyland Titan TD3c of 1934. One of eight front-entrance Harrington-bodied 'luxury' buses, No 344 (BKK 308) was the first new oil-engined vehicle in the M&D fleet. Note that the registration number is repeated where one might expect to see the M&D scroll displayed. The batch was originally purchased for use on the popular Maidstone–Folkestone service 10. *Alan Townsin collection*

At Les Pearson's Transport House Café is the M&D Strike Band, a 12-piece ensemble formed in 1936 at Hastings to drum up support and cash for trade-union recognition within the company. They were well-organised, as the 'button staff' with collecting tins suggest. This time the company acceded, and trade-union membership became the norm. One of the biggest fans of the band proved to be George French, no less! *Jack E. Baker*

thereafter took pride of place in their Kentish yeoman's house at Goudhurst.

Meanwhile, times were a'changing among the workforce. Tilling & BAT's response to the growing tide of pressure for trade-union recognition was met with 'Bill Jones Cards' (which, in short, advised the men how to please their employers) slipped into the weekly wage packets. M&D personnel sought the right to join the Transport & General Workers' Union, and were prepared to engage in periodical withdrawals of labour to achieve it.

The button staff took the lead in 1936, those at Hastings being the best-organised, basing themselves upon Les Pearson's 'Transport House Café' as their strike headquarters. They wore uniform, carried collecting tins and, to attract a crowd, formed a 12-piece brass band and developed a good repertoire in martial music. The threat of dismissal was this time aired but not implemented. By the summer of 1939 even the personnel at Postley Works, where engagement had long been subject to a ban on union membership, had been permitted to join the TGWU. The enrolment of many of its new members into the armed forces blunted the union's success somewhat, but it, like most others, proved anxious to participate fully in the drive toward military (rather than immediate social) victory.

George French too had mellowed. He made a point of going to Hastings to tell the strikers' brass band that he liked their music very much indeed, and 'would they please keep it on'! And, until wartime commitments whittled it away, they did so.

3. BET's M&D

During World War 2 (1939–45), petroleum products, even for commercial use, were rationed, and the 'black-out', followed by a 9.30pm curfew, eliminated numerous journeys. So too did the establishment of prohibited areas, enemy air activity (and coastal shelling at Folkestone) and the military impressment of company vehicles. Manufacturers going over to wartime production also caused a severe reduction in replacement buses, which in turn led to a struggle to keep a diminished fleet upon the road. The concentration of traffic in heavily-populated areas, meanwhile, meant many more passengers carried for fewer miles travelled. Conductresses again replaced men called up for military service. Maidstone & District's garage at Gillingham was hit on the night of 27 August 1940: three employees were killed and an estimated 51 vehicles were burned out. The Luftwaffe also destroyed M&D's office at Hastings and brought down sections of overhead equipment. M&D responded by forming the 26th Kent (Bus)

Battalion, Home Guard, in conjunction with the Royal Army Service Corps, and by transferring its company headquarters to Tunbridge Wells in October 1941.

In September 1942 Tilling & British Automobile Traction Ltd was wound up, and Maidstone & District was one of the operating companies allotted to BET. The partition saw Tilling's J. Frederick Heaton replaced upon the board by BET's Raymond Birch and, incidentally, enabled M&D to retain its traditional livery for another 30 years.

Col Humphrey Robinson died on 12 March 1945. His spectacular funeral at Crockham Hill Church was attended by leading figures in the transport industry, members of the Old Surrey & Burston Hunt, and of his regiment in No 1 dress, uniformed M&D inspectors, a firing party and the band of the Royal West Kent Regiment — quite a send-off for a busman. BET's Sidney Garcke became M&D Chairman in his stead until May 1946, when he stood aside in favour of Raymond P. Beddow — Chairman for the next 21 years (the record for M&D), giving it up in March 1968 only because the Transport Holding Co gained control upon nationalisation.

A fierce opponent of state-ownership in general, Beddow watched in dismay as, on 1 January 1948, the main-line railway companies (including the Southern's one-third share in Maidstone & District) were nationalised — and in some disbelief as Thomas Tilling Ltd sold up and followed suit the same year. He conducted a vociferous campaign in support of BET's 'no surrender' stance, which meant that Maidstone & District and its fellow BET companies would remain two-thirds un-nationalised for a further 20 years.

In the latter part of World War 2 16 Bristol-built T2-type anthracite-burning trailers were sent by M&D to the relatively flat Isle of Sheppey, where they were attached to elderly vehicles, so that they could run on gas, to save precious petrol supplies for the war effort. Nos 207 and 246 (KJ 1901/40) were two of the Leyland TD1 Titans which ran from Sheerness — but still found the going difficult on Minster Hill. *Alan Lambert collection*

The winter of 1946/7 was a particularly severe one, and many roads in Kent became impassable. No 710 (FKO 52), a 1939 Leyland Tiger TS8 single-decker, is lodged fast in a 3ft snowdrift near Wouldham. The 34-seat bodywork was by Eastern Coach Works of Lowestoft, successor to Eastern Counties, which earlier bodied some Tilling-Stevens saloon buses for M&D. *Ian Allan Library*

In June 1947 George Flexman French announced his forth-coming retirement from 'his' beloved M&D. However, his ex-secretary (and second wife) Florence 'Flip' French was of the opinion that 'he probably wouldn't have done so if he had known that M&D would survive nationalisation at that time'. Although he was 66, with his rank of Managing Director (since 1945) and his history of service, no one would have insisted upon his going. His last official act was to draw up preliminary plans for a new bus station and garage at Sandhurst Road, Hawkhurst (opened in June 1950). 'He was very proud of that . . . sometimes when he said he'd take me out for the day, he'd go around to see how all the depots were getting on . . . Even in the last few years of his life, he always called in at the Tenterden depot, even though he'd been retired 20 years . . . He'd spent his life with buses — he just adored them!'

French's retirement coincided with that of his 'Assistant' Engineer, H. O. Hallas. Thus, from within the ranks, Don Marshall was appointed M&D's first 'Chief Engineer'. It fell to him also to be responsible for the company's drivers (conductors being the responsibility of the Traffic Department). His main task included

every aspect of engineering, new rolling stock and specifications for bodywork, and the planning of buildings and supervision of their construction, in conjunction with BET's architect. In 1951 the latter included the extension of the bus station in Maidstone and improvements at Sheerness. Marshall was of the opinion that 'the postwar equipment at Postley Works was no longer of the best. The works were not really large enough and so we did more work at the depots than many other companies. Yet we were self-sufficient, and only road-springs were put to outside contract.'

Among the first postwar deliveries of vehicles were the remainder of the double-deck trolleybuses for Hastings Tramways. All were now 56-seaters, the first 15 from Sunbeam and the remaining 10 from AEC; bodywork was again divided between Park Royal and Weymann. The remaining Guy double-deckers and all but four of the single-deck trolleybuses were withdrawn, elevating the Hastings Tramways trolleybus fleet to 'the smartest in the country'. One old double-decker survived to become the most famous trolleybus (and later ex-trolleybus) on the South Coast, 'Happy Harold'.

Recognisably built to the same design credited to George French and his engineering colleagues in the 'Thirties, the Harrington 32-seat bodywork on this 1947 AEC Regal coach was originally built for express work. In this photograph, No CO22 (JKM 422) wears the 'reversed' livery introduced to the whole coach fleet from November 1948. The slot beside the side light is a 'trafficator', which preceded the indicator. *R. N. Hannay collection*

The Ian Allan 1950 booklet *abc Maidstone & District* carried upon its cover a very fine coloured scraperboard image, by A. N. Wolstenholme, of what then seemed to be a revolutionary new coach with a flat front. No CO116 (KKK 855), at Victoria Coach Station, is one of the startling newcomers — an AEC Regal III with 32-seat front-entrance bodywork by Harrington. *R. N. Hannay collection*

On the short run from Tonbridge to Lower Hayesden is No TS3 (LKP 44), one of four Dennis Falcon saloons with 20-seat bodywork by the chassis manufacturer, seen operating on route 132, one of those services acquired from Arthur Ashby's 'Ashline' of Tonbridge on 8 September 1948. All four were purchased in 1950 to work principally upon those routes. *R. N. Hannay collection*

In 1951 Maidstone & District took delivery of NKN 650, numbered (on paper) LC1 but always known as 'The Knightrider'. A Commer Avenger with 16-seat Harrington bodywork, it was intended solely for private-hire duties. The company's publicity material, from which this posed shot is taken, quoted no less a publication than the *New York Times* in describing it as 'the most luxurious of all coaches in Britain today'. The provision of air conditioning, armchair seats and cocktail cabinet meant this claim was not without justificaton. *Colin Morris collection*

Leyland Tiger TS7 coach No 558 (DKT 16), renumbered CO558 in 1950 and C558 in 1961, as petrol engines disappeared from the fleet, served the company long and well. New in 1937, it was rebodied by Harrington in 1950, its roof incorporating full-length racks for the carriage of band instruments. It was photographed at Knightrider House, Maidstone, in 1964, still looking good just prior to withdrawal.
M. R. Hodges collection

In 1950 Maidstone & District purchased examples of the Bristol L saloon bus, bodied, in standard Tilling fashion, with coachwork by Eastern Coach Works and thus, for M&D, looking rather unusual. No SO62 (MKN 211) was an LL5G, being the longer-wheelbase version with a Gardner five-cylinder engine, and was fitted with a 39-seat body.
M&D and East Kent Bus Club

All-Leyland Titan PD2/12
No DH389 (NKT 885) was
delivered in June 1951 —
one of an initial batch of 36
such buses, with an impressive
new engine produced by
Leyland as a result of
experience gained building
tank power-units in World
War 2. Fitted with a rear door
by Maidstone & District
in 1954, the bus was
photographed at Hawkhurst
in September 1966.
M. R. Hodges collection

Conventional buses were not quickly forthcoming, however, as manufacturers took longer than expected to re-tool for peacetime production. Many elderly prewar vehicles were obliged to soldier on well beyond their planned sell-by dates. Chassis lasted better than bodywork in many instances, and there was a major programme of replacement or reconstruction. Between 1949 and 1955 over 50% of the pre-1945 fleet was refitted in this way.

George French's post of General Manager went to Percy Graefe, who had been Secretary of M&D since 1914. The vacant post of Secretary went to Graefe's assistant since 1927, John Dixon. Another who rose to full office in 1947 was K. W. P. Kitson, who was appointed Traffic Manager upon the retirement of T. W. Marsh MBE, Traffic Superintendent since 1915. A noteworthy addition to the board in 1949 was Percival Stone-Clark (a BET appointee), who served as Managing Director from 1955 to 1957.

In the year ending March 1951, M&D's fleet exceeded 800 vehicles for the first time. The subsidiary Hastings and Chatham fleets comprised 50 and 52 respectively. Total mileage that year was 29,665,000, representing the boom time for the industry. In 1953 the share capital went from £1 million, where it had stood since 1936, to its maximum of £1,700,000. Following regulation in 1930, bus fares had remained largely unaltered, but the Finance Act 1950 let slip the leash: in April 1951 M&D and its subsidiaries were among those operators seeking, for the first time, to raise their fares.

The conductor's ticket rack was phased out of service in 1948 (Hastings Tramways following in 1950). Latterly it held Setright tickets of the insert type, but the introduction of the Setright Speed system, where the machine printed the data on an inserted paper roll, put paid to that. The new system was brought into use on a

joint service (122) with Southdown, started on 6 June 1948 between Gravesend, Tunbridge Wells and Brighton. Crews exchanged at Tunbridge Wells, and only the buses and some of their passengers went into 'foreign' territory. At 63 miles, it was claimed to be the longest stage-carriage service in the country.

A new bus station at Lower Stone Street, Maidstone, opened on 10 December 1951. Unlike the old bus station — now known as 'Mill Street' — this allowed buses to run in and out without backing into the platforms. The opening was a low-key affair, in deference to an horrific event six days previously:

On the dark winter's evening of 4 December 1951, a Chatham & District bus ran into the rear of a platoon of Royal Marine cadets, marching unlit and three-abreast, along a roadway in Gillingham. Twenty-four youngsters were killed and others injured. The involvement of a Luton-based vehicle shook the

▲ No DH417 (NKT 913) was one of five Leyland PD2/3 Titans delivered to M&D in 1951, with 56-seat Leyland bodywork to the original postwar style. In some quarters they were called the 'King Alfred' Titans, since it was rumoured that they were an order diverted from that Winchester operator. This one has just passed beneath the railway viaducts at Strood on 22 April 1967, during its last year of service. *M. R. Hodges collection*

▲ Originally World War 2 utility double-deckers of 1944/5 vintage, DH72 (HKE 271), a Guy Arab II, and DH145 (HKE 853), a Bristol K6A, were rebodied with 56-seat Weymann coachwork to the same design in 1949 and 1953 respectively. They display their narrow (7ft 6in) construction effectively at Gillingham bus station on a sunny summer's day in August 1965. *M. R. Hodges collection*

No DH439 (RKP 920) was a 58-seat Weymann-bodied Leyland Titan PD2/12 delivered to Maidstone & District in November 1953, originally with an open platform, but fitted with a rear door by Weymann five years later. It has arrived at Tenterden on service 12 on 2 April 1966 at a time when it had just one more year of service left in M&D ownership. *M. R. Hodges collection*

Bristol K6A No DH138 (HKE 239) was delivered in 1945 with Park Royal bodywork, in the days before the decision to restrict supplies of Bristol vehicles to the nationalised ex-Tilling companies. Rebodied with this Weymann Orion 56-seat bodywork in 1954, it served with Maidstone & District until 1967, and was photographed at Gillingham on 29 October 1966. *M. R. Hodges collection*

staff of all three companies to the core. In the midst of grief for the bereaved, their thoughts went out immediately to the distressed driver, a man of 40 years' experience with Chatham & District. So too did those of many who wrote to both Maidstone and Luton depots from all parts of the United Kingdom. Words used in remembrance of 35 men of the three companies killed in World War 2 seem appropriate to the loss of those young lads: 'Man's desperate folly was not theirs, but their's the sacrifice'. And the other victim, the poor driver, remained inconsolable for the rest of his life.

But for the determination of Gillingham, Chatham and Rochester to hang on to their statutory rights to purchase all or part of the Chatham & District company, the latter would, in all probability, have been wound up by this time. Eventually M&D and its Chatham subsidiary were obliged to seek Parliamentary approval for such a move, and this was granted by the Chatham & District Act 1955. The Chatham company was merged with Maidstone & District Motor Services Ltd from 1 October 1955 — it being considered 'un-businesslike to have two separate companies in watertight compartments, each dealing with similar traffic'. From that date the staff received new M&D badges and the vehicles began to acquire the dark Brunswick green livery.

A new General Manager was on hand to supervise the merger. Percy Graefe retired at the end of 1954, to be replaced by the former manager of South Wales Transport Co Ltd, William M. Dravers. He encountered problems: a dispute about employment conditions, notably the arrangement of road crews' shifts,

◄ In August 1953 the owners of the old-established firm of Skinner's (in its final guise as Skinner Luxury Coaches Ltd of St Leonards-on-Sea) sold its business and 11 coaches to Maidstone & District. The original firm had started with motor wagonettes in 1901. Among the coaches acquired was this one-off AEC Regal IV (FDY 246) with Gurney-Nutting bodywork, which became C122 with M&D but retained its original livery. It is seen at Ashford garage on 23 August 1965. *M. R. Hodges collection*

▼ A very unusual vehicle developed by Saunders-Roe in conjunction with Maidstone & District's own engineers was this semi-chassisless saloon bus, seen undergoing pavé road-tests before delivery in October 1953. No SO68 (RKE 540) had 43-seat bodywork, also by Saunders-Roe, that firm's better-known manufacturing skill post-World War 2. There were no further orders. *Ian Allan Library*

▲ When the Chatham & District fleet was absorbed into that of M&D in October 1955, 54 vehicles were involved. Among the more modern was this Guy Arab IV with 58-seat Weymann bodywork, which became No DH452 (RKK 992). It was less than two years old. The vehicle continued to serve in the Medway area, and was receiving some tender loving care at Gillingham on 27 April 1968.
M. R. Hodges collection

At Cobham terminus on a Saturday (9 July 1966) working is No DH475 (VKO 999), a Guy Arab IV with lightweight 60-seat Weymann Orion bodywork. One of eight originally ordered for the Chatham & District fleet, it was instead delivered, in December 1955, in full Maidstone & District livery, following the absorption of C&D.
M. R. Hodges collection

Among the vehicles (in C&D livery) taken over by M&D from the Chatham & District subsidiary were GKE 83, a 1939 Bristol K5G with 54-seat Weymann bodywork, and TKM 355, a Guy Arab IV, also with Weymann body, pictured at the Luton Road depot in Chatham. Both sport their new M&D fleetnumbers — DH304 and DH461 respectively. *M. R. Hodges collection*

No 6738 (VKR 38) was delivered in 1956 as No DL38, one of eight AEC Regent V MD3RV models with comparatively rare lowbridge Park Royal bodywork (hence the 'DL' prefix in the original fleetnumber). This was one of the last half-cab vehicles of this pattern to serve with Maidstone & District. Looking rather squat, it stands at Tenterden on 27 April 1968.
M. R. Hodges collection

Standing tall in comparison with its lowbridge sister of the same 1956 intake of AEC Regent V double-deckers, Park Royal-bodied No 5478 (VKR 470) also provided three extra seats. It was originally numbered DH478, being renumbered in 1968.
On route 29 bound for Maidstone on 10 September 1971, it has paused in Aylesford.
M. R. Hodges collection

In 1956 Maidstone & District took delivery of 15 additional examples of coaches incorporating chassis parts of AEC Regal III coaches of the late 'Forties, part of a total order for 23 vehicles. Beadle of Dartford was the builder engaged for such work during the 'Fifties. Beadle-AEC No CO370 (WKM 370) was a 37-seater introduced to help with an expanding express-coach programme. *Alan Townsin collection*

led to those at Gillingham banning rest-day work and overtime, coming out on strike for a short period when inspectors were instructed to act as conductors. By September 1955 passenger numbers were down by some 250,000 per month, compared with the previous year. A Government increase in fuel tax led to another increase in fares, and local people bought bicycles and scooters to avoid paying the higher fares — and they began staying at home in the evenings to watch their new (black-and-white) television sets. Meanwhile, machines for hop-picking greatly reduced the traditional influx of pickers from London each September, while unprecedented traffic congestion in Maidstone and the Medway Towns gave notice that a more affluent populace was beginning to buy motor cars in goodly numbers as well.

Until August 1950, M&D's only interest in Edenbridge was that it was the westerly point of circular service 93 from Tunbridge Wells. Then T. W. Smith of Edenbridge sold his AEC Regal coach to the company, which retained it there together with its driver, P. F. Franklin — M&D's sole representative. On 25 March 1951

Southdown Motor Services Ltd acquired the goodwill of H. J. Sargent's 'East Grinstead Services' — from that Sussex town to Cowden Cross, to Ashurst Wood, and from Edenbridge to Crowborough. Southdown employed Sargent's drivers and ran the services, together with ex-Sargent tours based upon Edenbridge and Westerham, until September of that year, when, under a BET-brokered deal, they were passed to Maidstone & District. This brought Edenbridge one more M&D service in addition to the now company-operated tours; a coach was outstationed in Oxted to cover the Westerham tours. A small depot (capacity 12 vehicles) was opened by M&D on 12 January 1955 in Hever Road. Remarkably (by today's standards), by November 1955 the company saw fit to employ 24 members of staff to run this, its 18th depot, with the local fleet size just seven vehicles.

Other building work at this time included the provision of new garage accommodation at Ashford and the reconstruction of the depot at Borough Green. Plans were also laid for the rebuilding of the garage at Sittingbourne, eventually completed in 1959.

▲ Entering service in 1957 as
No SO217, No 3217 (XKT 994)
was a 42-seat Weymann-bodied
AEC Reliance MU3RV saloon,
one of 12 ordered the previous
year. It was equipped from the
beginning for one-man operation
and served with the company
in its original livery until
withdrawal in 1970. It is pictured
in Wainscott, to the north of
Strood, on 6 September 1969.
M. R. Hodges collection

▲ On the Bensted House Hospital service at Faversham in July 1966
is an example of the classic M&D single-deck bus of the BET era.
The vehicle is No S224 (YKR 224), one of seven 42-seat Beadle-
bodied AEC Reliance MU3RV saloons delivered in the summer of
1957 for one-man operation. This was Beadle's 'Chatham' model.
M. R. Hodges collection

On the bus destination board:

SO OTHER SIDE FOR ROUND THE TOWN TOURS

1/6

VIA SEA FRONT,
ST. LEONARDS GDS.
MAZE HILL,
SHORNDEN WOOD,
ALEXANDRA PARK,
HASTINGS CASTLE,
OLD TOWN,
ALL SAINTS STREET,
FISH MARKET.

COMMENCING 1-30 FROM FISH MARKET.
EVERY 30 MINUTES.

1/6 ⊙ ROUND THE TOWN TOURS

HKL 826

In 1957 the South East Area Traffic Commissioners approved a Maidstone & District/Southdown co-ordination scheme called the 'Heathfield Cycle', which came into operation on 2 June. Services from Heathfield to Brighton, Uckfield, Tunbridge Wells, Hawkhurst, Hastings and Eastbourne were involved, and provision was made for the existing practice of bus manning by crews of either company. Against the national trend, services operated jointly were doubled and some fares were reduced.

Maidstone & District had already decided to prepare for one-man operation, initially referring to such a vehicle as an 'OMB'. Since double-deckers were still of half-cab configuration, only saloons were involved at first. The co-operation of the union was secured by a commitment that no conductor would be made redundant without being offered retraining for the new role. Thus M&D became one of the first operators to have over half its fleet comprising 'OMBs'.

William Dravers was General Manager for just two years. In June 1957 he was replaced by Arthur J. White from Devon General. The genial Mr White was to remain in office for 15 years. He too was confronted by a strike — a national dispute about higher wages for road crews — at the end of July 1957. The crews got a pay rise, but the fares had to go up again.

The Hastings Corporation Act 1937 had empowered the County Borough to purchase the whole Hastings Tramways trolleybus system, even if Bexhill did not wish to participate. Hastings very nearly did so in 1945. It could not afford it in 1950, and in 1955 the full Council decided not to accept its Transport Committee's recommendation for purchase. Bexhill also decided not to take over the section within its own boundaries. With effect from 1 October 1957, Hastings Tramways Co, together with its staff, premises, equipment and 46 trolleybuses, was merged with M&D. The vehicles received M&D fleetnames, and the staff exchanged

▲ Awaiting customers on Hastings seafront on 7 September 1966 is No OR2 (HKL 826), an AEC Regal O662 delivered in 1946 with Beadle saloon bodywork as No SO16. It served for 11 years in that role before being altered to this open style as a tourist attraction for 'round the town tours' — one of three so modified. Passengers were treated to a stage-by-stage commentary for their 1s 6d (7½p) fare. *M. R. Hodges collection*

their HTC badges for those of the parent company. The trolleybuses survived for a further 20 months.

In January 1959 the first M&D Leyland Atlantean PDR1/1 rear-engined double-decker, No DL43 (43 DKT) arrived in Hastings to familiarise trolleybus drivers with this free-ranging diesel-engined type. A fleet of 50 had been ordered to replace the trolleybuses. In preparation for their introduction, Bexhill went so far as to lower the roadway under the Sackville Railway Arch — previously for single-deckers only — and 14 lowbridge Atlanteans were ordered for that route as a result. The last trolleybus services were run on 31 May 1959.

The most notorious bridge on the M&D system, however, was the low railway arch adjacent to the old 58ft-span bridge across The Swale to the Isle of Sheppey. Equally difficult was the narrow and twisting approach road across the marshes. The latter was replaced by Sheppey Way, a broad highway cutting straight across, and a new 90ft-wide elevated bridge enabled double-deckers to reach the island without the need to dismantle them or use a 'private road' through Kemsley Mills and Ridham Dock. Driver G. T. White took the first M&D vehicle, a 60-seater Atlantean double-decker coach, across it on 29 February 1960.

Considerable and rapid housing development had taken place in the Tonbridge area, providing a valuable source of revenue. To meet the demand, a new depot was built in the town between Quarry Hill Road and St Mary's Road. An offshoot of Tunbridge Wells depot, it incorporated a new booking office and a garage for 36 vehicles, its roof being of reinforced concrete barrel vaults. Its initial fleet of 26 buses, in which Bristol saloons and double-deckers were well represented, required 50 drivers and 45 conductors, most transferred from Tunbridge Wells, where overcrowding was promptly eliminated. Tonbridge depot opened for business on 1 January 1961.

In August 1962, some 20 years after the company's Hastings office in Castle Street was destroyed in World War 2, M&D got a new and permanent replacement. Designed by BET architect H. A. F. Spooner, the accommodation consisted of a staff room in the basement, a booking and enquiry office on the ground floor, and two floors above with offices for the chief inspector and for District Superintendent David Meredith. The site had been occupied by an extremely small temporary structure used by inspectors. It was not until January 1963, however, that the last of the company's air-raid shelters, those at Knightrider House, Maidstone, were demolished.

Travelling along St Leonards Road, Bexhill-on-Sea, is No SO242 (242 BKM), an AEC Reliance MU3RV with 42-seat Harrington bodywork. The picture was taken in March 1958, when the vehicle was a very new addition to the Maidstone & District fleet, having entered service the previous January. AEC buses were well-represented locally, several Regent Vs included.
Ian Allan Library

60

No 6447 (47 DKT) was one of the celebrated batch of 14 Leyland Atlantean PDR1/1 double-deckers with lowbridge 73-seat Weymann bodywork originally sent to Hastings to help prepare for replacement of the trolleybus system. When delivered in 1959, it was numbered DL47. The vehicle is departing Hastings for Eastbourne, in Southdown territory, on 5 September 1970. *M. R. Hodges collection*

The classic M&D cream 'moustache' on the dash well to the fore, No DH494 (494 DKT) was a Leyland Atlantean PDR1/1 with full-height 78-seat Metro-Cammell bodywork. On 9 July 1967 it was working the main Hoo–Gillingham route, having just passed beneath a now long-gone military railway bridge at Four Elms Hill, Chattenden. The bus was renumbered 5494 the following year. *M. R. Hodges collection*

The play of light and shade in the sunshine, for which the attractive spa of Tunbridge Wells is well known, is momentarily disturbed by the passage of a 30-seat saloon, one of 15 such small-capacity Albion Nimbus NS3N models bodied by Harrington. New in 1960, as No SO310, No 3310 (310 LKK) was caught by the camera on 30 May 1970, just before its retirement from service. *M. R. Hodges collection*

On 1 July 1966 Harold Wilson's Labour Government permitted 'a more extensive use of one-man-operated buses'. But at Maidstone & District, the total demise of the conductor did not come about whilst the company was still under BET control.

The 'Sixties marked the end of an era, not just for the British Electric Traction Co, but for several individuals long associated with M&D. Among them were some stalwarts whose contributions had been outstanding. They included Horace 'Freddie' Fridd, then aged 70, who drove his last bus into Gillingham depot on 17 September 1966 after 52 years, 3 months and 11 days' service — an all-time record for an employee who had worked solely for M&D.

George Flexman French died on 19 January 1967, aged 86. He had continued to attend company functions until the last days of 1966. Raymond Beddow, no longer in the best of health, made his last Chairman's Address to shareholders at Knightrider House on 18 July 1967. Twenty years on, nationalisation threatened once again — and Beddow remained totally opposed to it.

As with other regional companies, completely or partially nationalised, M&D had suffered a steady decline in profits. For some while it had been unable to make any appropriation to the general reserve. Car ownership had increased apace, but the Wilson Government had proved no more inclined to remove the taxation suffered by the bus industry than had the previous Conservative administration. By 1967 the company was paying out some £328,000 annually in Fuel Tax, the operating profit was subject to Corporation Tax at 40%, and, on what dividends could be distributed, income tax removed 8s 3d (41¼p) in the pound.

The cyclical problem of increased prices and wages, leading to increased fares, had to be coped with as the number of passengers continued to decline — a situation seen by management as hastened by the introduction of a national 40-hour week in 1966.

It was against this background nationally that Sir John Wills, Chairman of the British Electric Traction Co Ltd, finally agreed to sell the group's road passenger interests in the United Kingdom. That decision was announced 'under pressure from Government', according to Sir John, on 22 November 1967. The general reaction of the trade press was that BET was doing well to be paid for a leaking vessel. The BET subsidiaries, Maidstone & District included, were transferred to the Transport Holding Co, set up by the Government at the beginning of 1963 as successor to the BTC, on 14 March 1968.

In May 1951, Maidstone & District purchased the Hastings-based business and four vehicles of J. C. Bingham's Scout Motor Coaches. The acquired fleet of coaches was operated briefly, but the name and the red and white livery were applied thereafter to some of M&D's coaches. No CO444 (444 LKE) was a Harrington-bodied AEC Reliance 2MU3RV of 1960 which served in the Scout colours. *M. R. Hodges collection*

Specially ordered for service in Hastings and delivered in 1963 were 10 AEC Reliance 2MU2RA saloon buses with 42-seat Harrington bodywork. Built to the old 7ft 6in width (8ft by now being the norm), these one-man-operated buses were required in the area for routes with particularly tight traffic conditions. No S199 (199 XKE) departs from Hastings on 7 September 1966. *M. R. Hodges collection*

63

Collecting passengers for Maidstone on 2 April 1966 at Tenterden is an AEC Reliance 2U3RA with 53-seat bodywork by Weymann. No S50 (EKJ 110C) was at that time still crewed by a conductor in addition to the driver. It became No 3750 in the 1968 renumbering scheme which dispensed with letter prefixes in 1968, and was converted for one-man operation the following year. *M. R. Hodges collection*

Representing the last of a famous line of Harrington-bodied coaches operated by M&D is AEC Reliance 2U3RA No C58 (FKL 121D), a beautiful Grenadier coach delivered together with 14 others in 1965 but stored until the spring of the following year, when they were first registered. It is seen at Knightrider Street garage, Maidstone, soon after entering service. *M. R. Hodges collection*

At Hastings on 5 September 1970 (NBC days, really) are two M&D buses still in BET green. Working the London express service was Atlantean No 5621 (621 UKM), despite its ordinary bus seats. In contrast, luxurious No 4625 (VKN 625J), a Leyland Leopard PSU3A/4R with 48-seat Duple Commander IV bodywork, was one of the last six M&D coaches to enter service in BET colours. *M. R. Hodges collection*

4. NBC's M&D

Largely as a holding exercise, pending replacement of the Transport Holding Co with something more substantial, Richard Ellery, an ex-BET man, was appointed Chairman of M&D. Peter Yorke and Jim Skyrme joined the board as representatives of THC. The latter became Chairman for one year in 1969, following Ellery's departure.

The National Bus Company, which came into being on 1 January 1969, was staffed at below-Chairman level by executives drawn from the BET and ex-Tilling groups. It chose to operate through its existing subsidiaries. Each of those, including Maidstone & District, remained technically a limited-liability company by virtue of just one of its shares' being held by a nominee of NBC. Profits, if any, now accrued to the National Bus Company.

From the outset, NBC divided itself into operational regions. Financial constraints led to considerable pack-shuffling in this quarter, but, as originally organised, M&D found itself allocated, together with Brighton Hove & District, East Kent, Southdown

and Timpson & Sons, to the South Eastern Region, under the chairmanship of Jim Skyrme. When he became Chief Executive of NBC in January 1971, the first adjustment to the regional structure was made. This reduced the original nine regions to six, and re-grouped M&D and its South Eastern fellows with the Southern Region (Aldershot & District, City of Oxford, Hants & Dorset, Gosport & Fareham, Shamrock & Rambler, Southern Vectis and Thames Valley). Chairman of the enlarged Southern Region was David S. Deacon, who, despite his Tilling origins, now became Chairman also of Maidstone & District. To its credit, NBC now set the precedent for the automatic appointment to the boards of its subsidiaries of serving general managers. Thus Arthur White became an M&D director in 1969, which was more than BET had done for him or his predecessors Percy Graefe and William Dravers.

By December 1970 M&D was among those NBC subsidiaries which had submitted to local authorities lists of rural services which required subsidies if their operation were to continue.

There was a rapid transformation from a position of staff shortage to one where it became necessary to terminate the employment of some drivers and conductors. Meanwhile, M&D was obliged to carry out the upgrading of its premises. In 1971 the Bexhill office received a face-lift, and the considerable reconstruction and modernisation of Luton depot was completed. Together with a continuing decline in the number of passengers carried, these factors contributed toward Maidstone & District's first-ever financial loss, in the year 1970/1. There followed NBC's decision to introduce a corporate image — and that too proved a costly business.

Arthur J. White retired in 1972, to be replaced in June by Leonard

◀◀ Parked together at Sittingbourne railway station on 12 August 1972 are No 3433 (AKM 433K), a 'short' Leyland Leopard PSU4A/2R with Willowbrook bodywork, and No 5602 (602 UKM), a Weymann-bodied Leyland Atlantean PDR1/1. The former is providing part of the town service before striking out for Milstead. In contrast, the Atlanteans worked the long Faversham–Gravesend service — the major cross-Medway route. *M. R. Hodges collection.*

◀ Whilst the new National Bus Company found its feet, the subsidiary companies were able to carry on their daily routines more or less undisturbed. Some tried new fleetname styles, but M&D simply moved their time-honoured scroll forward on some saloon buses, to a position above the wheel arch. No 3402 (UKE 402H), a Leyland Leopard with Marshall bodywork, demonstrates the style on service in Tunbridge Wells. *Edward Shirras / Ian Allan Library*

Higgins, with the newly created rank of Chief General Manager (of the Channel Coast companies: Southdown, Maidstone & District and East Kent). As NBC's leaf-green and white livery replaced the dark Brunswick green and broken white, he dutifully forecast that 'this will brighten-up the company's image'. Not too many at M&D agreed with that, particularly since the coach fleet came under the control of NBC's Central Activities Group and was repainted white overall.

One of Len Higgins' earlier responsibilities was to supervise the managerial unification of Maidstone & District and the East Kent Road Car Co Ltd. In 1973 M&D took over East Kent's services in the Rye area and, later, those around Faversham. M&D's activities in the Ashford area were transferred to East Kent. East Kent's headquarters at Canterbury was chosen as the location for the joint traffic departments, whilst Maidstone became responsible for the secretarial and accounts departments. The transfer of engineering work to Canterbury in 1974 led to an attempt to establish a common fleet-numbering scheme, but widespread speculation about a total merger under a new identity proved fruitless. Staff, passengers and local authorities were assured, in a formal statement, that both companies would retain their identities and separate liveries, rationalisation being the sole aim of the exercise.

Some financial relief for M&D was forthcoming as a result of a provision in the Local Government Act 1972. This obliged counties to grant subsidies to local transport operators for the continued provision of unremunerative (mostly rural) bus services. In M&D's case the counties were Kent and East Sussex. Despite the problems, by February 1974 M&D had purchased nine coaches from T. G. Cox of Maidstone (fleetname 'Streamline') and followed that in May by acquiring the licences, six dual-purpose and two saloon buses of John Dengate & Sons based at Rye in Sussex.

One of 10 Leyland Panthers delivered for use at Hastings was in NBC's leaf-green and white livery by October 1972, when this picture was taken. The traditional scroll remains, however, in its new location. No 3111 (LKT 111F) was a PSUR1/1R model with 45-seat Strachans bodywork fitted for one-man operation. In order to help shift the tourist traffic, the batch was fitted with dual doors.
Peter W. Robinson / Ian Allan Library

Even some of the double-deckers which had received their leaf-green and white livery still retained the scroll fleetname until NBC insisted otherwise. Just as sister company Southdown found any excuse to use its old-style fleetname, so the M&D workshops seemed reluctant to let go of company tradition. 1959-vintage Leyland Atlantean PDR1/1 No 5499 (499 DKT) was at Maidstone in October 1972. *M. R. Hodges collection*

In June 1973 No 3754 (EKJ 114C), an AEC Reliance 2U3RA with 53-seat Weymann bodywork, displays full NBC livery, complete with white NBC-style 'M&D' fleetname and 'double N' logo. The bus has stopped beside M&D's own 'Tudor Rose' building, which housed its booking office and a sub-let restaurant, at Tenterden — a town which William Cobbett said was home to the prettiest girls in the land. *M. R. Hodges collection*

An even more startling livery change befell the coach fleets of NBC's subsidiaries. The vehicles became all white with 'NATIONAL', in alternate red and blue letters, as the fleetname. For a short while 'Maidstone & District' appeared in grey letters over the front wheel-arch, underlined with a bar of M&D green to show fleet origin. No 2551 (BKT 814C), a Reliance with dual-purpose Weymann body, emerges in its white coat in July 1972.
M. R. Hodges collection

Another set of traditional 'Maidstone & District' scrolls has escaped from the workshops — rather unusually finding its way onto the flanks of a red bus. No 5001 (GCN 803G) was one of 12 Daimler Fleetline CRG6LX/Alexander 77-seaters part-exchanged in 1972 with Northern General Transport of Gateshead for a similar number of M&D single-deck Fleetlines. It is pictured in Eccles on 28 October 1972.
M. R. Hodges collection

An opportunity to admire a Maidstone & District double-decker bus in its full NBC glory — right down to the pale grey wheels — is provided by No 5710 (FKM 710L). Pictured at Maidstone when brand new, on 20 November 1972, the vehicle is a Leyland Atlantean PDR1A/1 Special, one of an order diverted to Maidstone & District from the intended customer, Midland Red. Perhaps the lady in red is its first-ever passenger. *M. R. Hodges collection*

During the NBC era there were very strong links between M&D and the East Kent Road Car Co Ltd, to the extent that many believed that the two companies would become one. Politics ensured that did not happen, but there were many vehicle exchanges and mutual loans. East Kent No 7961 (RFN 961G), a Daimler Fleetline CRG6LX/Park Royal 72-seater, was found working for M&D in Tunbridge Wells on 29 September 1978. *M. R. Hodges collection*

On 5 May 1974 Maidstone & District acquired the licences and eight single-deck vehicles of John Dengate & Sons, an old-established firm at Rye, Sussex. What became No 2853 in the M&D fleet (LJH 253L) continued to operate for some while in its original Dengate colours with NBC-style Maidstone & District fleetname. A 49-seat Willowbrook-bodied Leyland Leopard, it is seen at Rye on 18 May 1974.
M. R. Hodges collection

No 5382 (LKP 382P) was one of five Volvo-Ailsa B55-10 buses with 79-seat Alexander bodywork, evaluated by M&D for the National Bus Company in comparison with four Bristol VRTs and five Scania BR111DH double-deckers. The trials began in Hastings and then moved to Luton depot in Chatham, where No 5382 is seen at The Brook, Chatham, *en route* to Borstal on 2 April 1977. The Bristol VRT3 became NBC's standard double-decker.
B. L. Jackson / Ian Allan Library

In October 1975 the designated operating areas of M&D and East Kent were reduced to four. Maidstone & District's two were North West (Borough Green, Faversham, Gillingham, Gravesend, Luton, Maidstone, Sheerness and Sittingbourne) and South West (Hastings/Silverhill, Tenterden, Tonbridge, Tunbridge Wells, Bexhill and Hawkhurst), each under an Area Manager with responsibility for local secretarial, engineering and traffic departments. The retention of local goodwill was a primary objective. Len Higgins: 'Transport is essentially a local matter, and, in many problems, investigations and meetings with District and Parish Councils are more profitably handled by local officers of the company, who are better known in their localities than is possible for officials from Head Office.'

Despite some good reports about other types, NBC did not budge
from its choice of the Bristol VRT as its standard double-decker, and
Maidstone & District took the type in large quantities. At Tunbridge
Wells on 13 March 1982 is VRTSL6LX No 5803 (PKE 803M) of
1973, with ECW body; followed by an ex-South Yorkshire PTE
example with East Lancs bodywork, No 5775 (OWE 275K),
one of a batch of 12 acquired in 1980.
M. R. Hodges collection

In October 1980 Maidstone & District introduced its highly successful Invictaway pay-as-you-board coach service to London — from the Medway Towns, initially. Later a striking black livery was adopted for some vehicles, and three Leyland Leopards received the names of Dickensian characters (as befitted their Chatham base). No 2147 (BKJ 147T) became *Louisa Bounderby* — joined later by *Lucie Manette* (2152) and *Lizzie Hexham* (2153). *Ian Allan Library*

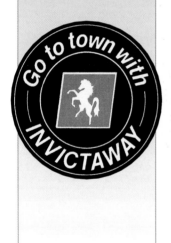

These gave M&D the opportunity to introduce pay-as-you-board coach services to London, marketed imaginatively as 'Invictaway'.

The original idea for what became the Invictaway service came from a 1978 meeting of traffic superintendents with M&D's North West Area Manager, held in the old windmill owned by Meopham Parish Council. Roger Davies: 'We used to run National Express coaches from Medway and Sheerness to London (003/005) . . . but the trouble with the National Express coaches was that you had to reserve a seat three days ahead at a booking office. With a train, it was down to the station, buy a ticket and get on a train. We thought that we must do something about this. Then the superintendent from Sheerness, George Digby, said

"What we need is a pay-as-you-enter coach service" . . . So we devised it, did a timetable and made some test runs with AEC Reliance No 2578 (HKT 578D) . . . That's how the company decided to try this "Invictaway" idea, and took it along to the next meeting with the railway . . . which, of course, said . . . "Travel to London is ours, and if you apply for a licence for that bus service, we shall object" . . . Along comes the 1980 Act and the key part was that the onus of proof was now upon the established operator to say why the new application should not be allowed — why it would damage their business.' Invictaway came into being on the very first day of enactment, 6 October 1980.

Started as a coach service for commuters, Invictaway quickly

built up to a half-hourly off-peak departure from the Medway Towns to Victoria Coach Station — probably the most frequent on that route, ever. Always a registered service, whereas competing operators' commuter services were 'unlicensed notified express', Invictaway was the only one which ran off-peak. M&D did not get into the commuter-coach business in a big way until Olson's Coaches gave up overnight, early in 1982. Invictaway rushed to fill the gap, by drafting in six coaches from East Kent and some from M&D garages. The service grew and grew, and the Invictaway brand was introduced also at Maidstone and at Tunbridge Wells. Roger Davies: 'Invictaway was important [also] in MAP terms, because in the very depressing days of the late

'Seventies and into MAP, when we were closing depots and making people redundant, Invictaway was a shining light of positiveness. It was growing, it was new, it was generating extra jobs, and therefore it was a very useful morale-booster.'

Whereas the National Bus Company had been engaged in a 'bigger the better' policy, the Conservative Government was quick to realise that the opposite would facilitate a simpler method of privatising the industry on a piecemeal basis. Accordingly, the M&D/East Kent marriage ended in divorce on 22 May 1983, and the former component had to find somewhere else for its headquarters. The chosen place was the office of the Area Manager, North West, at Luton Road, Chatham, where

office space had been available since the opening of the Pentagon Bus Station in 1976.

Although still under NBC control, the post-split M&D was, in effect, a new company. All members of senior management had to apply for posts in its fresh organisation — a process which took some five months. Technically, they had been temporarily dismissed, and were somewhat dismayed to discover that the buses just kept going normally with no problem, despite the fact that the senior management was, for the moment, 'absent'. The newly-appointed management team comprised Stephen Trennery (Managing Director), David Powell (Fleet Engineer), Eileen Lim (Finance Manager), Peter Baumann (Marketing Manager) and Roger Davies (Traffic Manager). Meanwhile Hastings & District, now re-defined to cover Hastings and Rye, became a separate NBC subsidiary company, thus restricting M&D bases to the county of Kent. In keeping with NBC 'wind-down' policy, a new non-operational company, Kent Engineering Ltd, was set up at Canterbury and Hawkhurst, and M&D's Postley Works closed on 11 June 1983.

Toward the end of its days, NBC became very keen to get its subsidiaries to adopt minibuses. A consultant sent to M&D to put together a marketing package came up with the name 'Minvictaway'. Instead, when M&D received its first minibuses,

it stuck to its 'Maidstone & District' fleetname. The first examples entered service at Sittingbourne in July 1986. Roger Davies: 'If anything, we were slightly cautious. We took 39 at first, and we could have done with a few more. We deliberately made them little M&D buses because of the strength of the marketing image . . . It was the first application of our changed style of fleetname, because we were then into the privatisation programme, so we began to drop the corporate NBC identity for our own style of fleetname. It was probably one of the most remarkable negotiations we ever had, getting the minibus-operating agreement agreed with the union, which took place in a Rochester hotel and lasted from 10am until 3am the following morning — and we came to an agreement.'

The Transport Act 1985 which came into force on 26 October 1986, known in the industry as 'Deregulation Day', created a world of free competition in the stage-carriage sector. Maidstone & District could now expect competition, especially as MABS had been forced to cease functioning from that day onward.

NBC had already planned and put in train the process of selling off its subsidiary companies, as required by Government. There was nothing to stop anyone who could realistically afford it from putting in a bid for any of those companies. The attention of the M&D management team was drawn to a line in the explanatory

literature about the possibility of 'management
buy-out', and the five officers of the team
decided to launch a bid. Picking at random
from a dictionary, they found the name of one
of the eight 'founder crops' which launched
agriculture around 9,000BC. Thus was
'Einkorn Ltd' formed to make the formal bid
for Maidstone & District Motor Services, its
registered office 9A Snodhurst Avenue, Chatham,
home of the M&D Traffic Manager. The money
markets were fascinated, and Einkorn was the
subject of much interest. But, in the event, the
necessary loans were arranged by the National
Westminster Bank — for very many years
M&D's bankers in Chatham.

The bid was formally announced during a
75th-anniversary celebration of the founding of
Maidstone & District at an hotel in Tunbridge
Wells. People who had been involved with the
company — suppliers, local authorities, the
'movers and shakers' of the area, and former
staff — were invited to lunch with the team and
were the first to hear the news.

Around the time of the break-up of the joint M&D/East Kent management at Canterbury and the removal of M&D headquarters to Chatham, there was something of a make-do-and-mend approach to vehicle intake. Among the one-off vehicles taken on board was this ex-Potteries Motor Traction Dennis Dominator DD102 with 74-seat low-height Alexander bodywork, No 5300 (XBF 700S), seen at Hoo School on 2 May 1984. *M. R. Hodges collection*

Despite NBC's love-affair with the Bristol VRT, M&D liked the Metrobus; when M&D was separated from East Kent, the first order placed by the former for double-deckers was for 10 Mark 2 versions — and it was very pleased with those also. No 5203 (A203 OKJ), a 77-seat DR102/42 model, is shown at The Pantiles, Tunbridge Wells, on 1 August 1984. *P. J. Wylie / Ian Allan Library*

At the curiously atmospheric Hawkhurst bus station on a wet day in December 1983 is No 3450 (EKJ 450K), a Leyland Leopard PSU4B/4R saloon with Marshall bodywork. The vehicle was delivered new in 1972 and had been converted in 1979 to carry 52 passengers. It served with Maidstone & District until 1987. At the time the photograph was taken, Kent Engineering Ltd was occupying the main building at Hawkhurst. *P. J. Noonan / Ian Allan Library*

During the run-up to deregulation and privatisation of the bus industry nationally, most NBC subsidiaries continued to take on board a goodly share of second-hand vehicles. Among those received by M&D were nine Dennis Dominator DD101A double-deckers with 75-seat East Lancs bodywork, new to East Staffordshire. In Railway Street, Chatham on 22 November 1986, No 5312 (PRE 35W) displays leaf-green livery with a '75 years of M&D' logo added. *Kevin Lane / Ian Allan Library*

As deregulation and privatisation approached, the main double-deck workhorse in the Maidstone & District fleet remained the Bristol VR. No 5116 (PKM 116R) was a VRTSL3/6LXB model with standard Eastern Coach Works body. Like other vehicles in the fleet, it lost its NBC identity a little early, with a new fleetname style, an 'M&D' vinyl over the 'double N' and a cream band, instead of white, to go with the retained leaf green. *Kevin Lane / Ian Allan Library*

For faithful service, however, No 2621 (621 UKM) took some beating. This was the 1963-vintage Weymann-bodied Leyland Atlantean PDR1/1 MkII bus which had (as No 5621) served as an express coach in its comparative youth. It became a member of the coach fleet proper in the 'Eighties as a schools private-hire vehicle known as 'Bertie the Bus' — still carrying its large fleetnumber on the roof to enable it to pop into the Pentagon Bus Station. It served M&D for 26 years. *D. E. Jenkins / Ian Allan Library*

5. Privatisation and After

Stephen Trennery and his colleagues were obliged to run a bus company, design a 'privatisation' business plan and prepare for deregulation and its likely aftermath, all at one and the same time. The process was being repeated elsewhere, but M&D proved to be the subject of an early sale. Chief among the imponderables was the outcome of provisions for unremunerative services. The County Council now had to put these out to competitive tender. How many tenders would it issue? How successful would M&D be? How much competition would arise? It speaks volumes for the expertise and judgment of the team that their estimate of how successful they would be in County Council tenders was within just one bus of the outcome.

The Einkorn bid was duly sent to NBC. There proved to be three other serious expressions of interest in M&D, one from a large French transport combine. The latter graciously withdrew, and the others made no formal bid. On 7 November 1986 the management buy-out team went to NBC headquarters, recently removed from New Street Square (off Fleet Street) to Buckingham Palace Road (Victoria Coach Station). The payment transferred and the documents signed, the Einkorn directors looked down from the office windows upon the Invictaway coaches beneath. They, and every other part of Maidstone & District Motor Services Ltd, were all theirs. The team comprised Stephen Trennery (Chairman and Managing Director), David Powell (Director of Engineering), Eileen Lim (Director of Finance), Peter Baumann (Director of Marketing) and Roger Davies (Director of Operations). The following February, M&D Advertising Ltd became an additional Einkorn subsidiary.

The premises inherited with the privatised M&D were: Nelson Road depot and bus station, Gillingham; Luton Road depot, Chatham; Bridge Street bus station, Sheerness (where a workshop would be added in 1990/1); East Street depot, Sittingbourne (closed in 1990 and replaced by Crown Quay Lane compound for the local M&D minibuses); Maidstone Road, Borough Green, depot (closed in 1992); Lower Stone Street bus station, Maidstone; lease of the Pentagon Bus Station, Chatham; St John's Road/Woodbury Park Road depot, Tunbridge Wells; Sandhurst Road bus station and depot, Hawkhurst; lease of a yard

On 7 November 1986 Maidstone & District Motor Services Ltd was purchased lock, stock and barrel from the National Bus Company by its senior management team of five. The formalities were completed at NBC headquarters in Victoria Coach Station. Pictured afterward on the step of a Leyland Olympian Invictaway coach are (left to right): Roger Davies, Eileen Lim, Stephen Trennery, Transport Minister David Mitchell, David Powell and Peter Baumann.
Roger Davies collection

Some rather nice old buses survived to become part of the independent and privatised Maidstone & District fleet. No 3445 (EKJ 445K), a Leyland Leopard PSU4B/4R with 45-seat Marshall bodywork of 1972, had been modified in 1979 to seat an extra seven passengers — and survived in M&D service until 1993. The vehicle shows very nicely how the addition of cream paint to the original NBC leaf green lifted the visual impact of the fleet. *Richard Lewis / Ian Allan Library*

Although adorned with less cream paint than the saloon buses and coaches, even the double-deckers looked much better in their new guise — especially since they sported a new M&D logo originally designed to cover up NBC's 'double N' device. This one, however, was a brand-new vehicle, a Leyland Olympian ONLXB/1RH, one of 10 taken on strength by the team in 1988. *Roger Davies collection*

A Leyland Tiger TRCTL11/3RH coach with 53-seat Plaxton Paramount 3500 3 bodywork, E187 XKO was new in 1988 as No 2187. It was photographed in 1992 as C187, bearing a livery which owed much to the latter-day NBC 'Venetian blind' style. Later, in 1995, this coach was repainted in Invictaway colours, in which it ran for a few months before it became a Green Line vehicle. *Roger Davies collection*

in Morley Road, Tonbridge (Quarry Hill Road having closed in 1982), and a yard at Lee Green, Tenterden.

Hawkhurst included the versatile workshop formerly run by Kent Engineering Ltd and inherited by M&D in 1985. Many of the staff had been transferred from Postley Works upon its closure. They were willing to tackle anything, built up much outside work from haulage companies and other bus operators — and badgered Head Office for a specimen of every type of vehicle owned by M&D, so that they could learn all about it.

The Lower Stone Street bus station in Maidstone was closed in 1988, at a time when the company believed that vehicles terminating in the town would be able to use a purpose-built replacement bus station — part of a town-centre development plan. Sadly that did not come about, but Maidstone Borough Council arranged for M&D's first association with its Armstrong Road depot by allotting parking facilities there that same year.

Einkorn Ltd acquired its third and final subsidiary on 22 June 1988. New Enterprise Coaches (Tonbridge) Ltd had competed locally against M&D following deregulation, but was in existence before that with a fleet of some 20 vehicles. Einkorn

purchased the goodwill and 17 vehicles, together with the services of Dennis Taylor, to continue running the operation. Although the licensed address removed to Luton Road, Chatham, and the Einkorn (M&D) directors became its new board, the firm was kept as a separate entity. Beside contract work, it was concerned with excursions and tours at a time when coach fleets among the ex-NBC companies were on the decline. On the grounds that coaching and buses no longer mixed too comfortably, its separation permitted the company to keep a foothold in that traditional area. Basically, Einkorn did not alter much at New Enterprise, but the latter benefited from buses cascaded from M&D, plus all the advantages of being associated with that company.

Post-MABS and deregulation, Maidstone Borough Transport (Holdings) Ltd, trading as 'Boro'line', competed as best it could, in the manner of the times, and took on some tendered work for London Transport, becoming somewhat overstretched in the process. Its troubles and financial ills were made public at Council meetings and widely reported in the press, and M&D management began to fear the ramifications in Maidstone if (or

Among the assets acquired by the buy-out team were the 39 Mercedes-Benz L608D minibuses with 20-seat Rootes bodywork built in Maidstone. Among the urban areas in which they busied themselves was Tonbridge, where Nos 1005/14 (C205/14 EKJ) were photographed on 10 June 1989. Maidstone & District's minibus services generated very few complaints from passengers. They were frequent: 'if you miss one there'll be another one in a few minutes'. *Kevin Lane / Ian Allan Library*

The independent Maidstone & District continued to take delivery of minibuses, moving on to the Mercedes-Benz 609D model in 1987. No 1076 (G76 PKR) was one of a batch of 19, with Reeve-Burgess panel-van-conversion bodies, delivered in the winter of 1989/90. *Ian Allan Library*

when) Boro'line collapsed, creating an unpredictable vacuum. Accordingly, Maidstone & District registered an urban network of its own in Maidstone, 'so that townspeople could become used to seeing and using green buses if Boro'line ceased to trade'. Rather than remain the tenant of an operator with which it was now competing, M&D removed its vehicles and staff from Armstrong Road and rented a yard, for some 20 buses, in Hart Street at the back of Maidstone West railway station. This roused the ailing Boro'line into action, and its buses turned up to compete in the Medway Towns, despite its financial difficulties. For five days, its vehicles went up into the Pentagon Bus Station in Chatham, causing congestion, until a High Court injunction required them to desist. For the last four months of its existence Boro'line ran against M&D whilst in receivership, but finally

gave up altogether at the end of May 1992. M&D did not buy Boro'line but purchased the Armstrong Road depot and its remaining 41 buses — all of which were sold on without entering the M&D fleet; it did, however, retain the breakdown truck. The move into the large full-scale Armstrong Road depot made feasible the closure that August of Borough Green depot, whose staff were retained.

Similar competitive activity was encountered at other locations, notably at Tunbridge Wells, but on a much smaller scale. There, in December 1991, M&D eventually purchased the local bus services and four Leyland saloon buses of Shearings Ltd.

Apart from its Invictaway vehicles, which really operated like long-distance stage-carriage buses, Maidstone & District's coach fleet diminished rapidly from the late 'Eighties onward, the

Navy Days! Having lost its former naval glory, the ancient seaport was delighted when HMS *Chatham* came to town for its commissioning ceremony in 1989. Invited guests were ferried to the ship's brow by the five brand-new Leyland Olympian ON2R50G13Z4 double-deckers with Northern Counties low-height 75-seat bodywork, specially chartered for the occasion. Company officers were obliged to return the White Ensign. *Roger Davies collection*

'Cheer-up for Chatham: Dover's in sight' (old naval saying). When HMS *Chatham* made a return visit to the port, Maidstone & District was presented by the Ship's Captain with a signed photograph of the vessel. He also admired the bus brought along for the occasion by the company's Director of Operations. This was No 3464 (J464 MKL), one of an initial batch of three Dennis Dart saloons with 40-seat Plaxton Pointer bodywork. *Roger Davies collection*

remainder being based largely at Gillingham depot. This decline coincided with a considerable slump in the popularity of coach tours and private hire, particularly in the South of England. At the same time, it was realised that a service bus can earn much more than a coach over a given period. Indeed, at privatisation M&D coaches were providing less than 5% of turnover.

Whilst Boro'line's difficulties were blamed by many councillors on its decisions to (a) conduct contractual operations for London Transport in Bexley and Greenwich and (b) go into the coaching business, it had been beset in September 1990 by another problem back in Maidstone. Bygone Buses of Biddenden had begun to compete against Boro'line with a fleet of 17 vehicles, at lower fares and frequencies, on its traditional routes. Maidstone & District was affected on radial routes but took no action against the newcomer. However, the struggle between Boro'line and Bygone Buses, particularly the alleged blocking of bus stops in Maidstone town centre, had a significant impact upon M&D's operations.

Following Boro'line's demise, M&D expected the congestion problem to

ease, but instead Bygone registered against M&D's service 12 in May 1992 and then its service 5. M&D responded with additional journeys and matched fares, making a number of complaints about blocking and other tactics to both the Traffic Commissioners and local authorities; it did not undercut Bygone's low fares or engage in predatory price behaviour. A fairly similar situation occurred in competition with the vehicles run by Turner's of Maidstone; again, competition was focused on profitable journeys rather than providing a full timetable over a given route. Since 1986, 15 other operators had entered the market in the traditional M&D area, five of which had departed by 1992. That November however, the M&D directors were dispirited and disillusioned to discover that a complaint had been made to the Office of Fair Trading, whose Director General referred the matter to the Monopolies & Mergers Commission. The enquiry, which lasted some six months, was directed solely at M&D, during which time the directors were obliged to gather together volumes of evidence as and when requested — and run a bus company. The Commission reported that some of the company's actions were deemed to be 'against the public

interest'. Draconian measures were imposed on M&D, restricting its ability to compete. Operations Director Roger Davies described it as 'being forced to fight with one hand tied behind our back', and felt so strongly about the matter that he resigned.

These events were watched with great interest by the industry. Groups which are now household names nationally were no doubt reinforced in their belief that the way forward was not by competition but by purchase and acquisition. Maidstone & District itself purchased the operations of Bygone on 29 May 1994, but its neighbours Hastings & District and East Kent had already been sold by their managements to Stagecoach, in December 1989 and September 1993 respectively. The Einkorn group duly placed its subsidiary companies on the market, and accepted the highest bid for all three. On 13 April 1995 they became the property of the British Bus group. British Bus closed down Maidstone & District's coaching activities in September, and, at the end of the month, M&D Advertising Ltd ceased trading.

The new Managing Director of Maidstone & District (and of New Enterprise) was John P. Piper, already Managing Director of Kentish Bus at Northfleet, purchased by British Bus in 1994.

From 1991 to 1993 a pair of Leyland Tigers carried Olau Line livery in connection with the ferry service from Sheerness to Vlissingen in Holland. This contract was worked as part of the Invictaway network, hence the logos. No 2173 (YSU 896, ex-A135 EPA) had 53-seat Plaxton Paramount 3200 Express bodywork, and was with London Country North East (paradoxically as a Green Line vehicle) before entering M&D service in 1991.
Roger Davies collection

With him came Justin Davies (Operations Director), Ian Tarran (Engineering Director) and Kevin Hawkins (Commercial Director), with Eileen Lim joining the team later as Finance Director. Following route exchanges between M&D and Kentish Bus, the latter's site at Gravesend and M&D's Luton Road premises were closed, and the two head offices were merged into one. This enabled Invictaway Ltd to be retained as a service company which ran the management of M&D, Kentish Bus and New Enterprise at Invicta House, Armstrong Road, Maidstone. The 'Invictaway' fleetname was replaced on the associated London express operations, which became part of the Green Line network in September 1995.

In June 1996 British Bus was bought by the Cowie group. Among other things, it was decided to take the M&D fleet livery in hand. Kevin Hawkins: 'The brief we gave the designer [Ray Stenning] was to update it and expand on the traditions of M&D: "That's what the M&D logo originally looked like — do a more modern interpretation of it".' For a very brief period indeed, as it turned out, M&D buses appeared in a colour scheme of deeper

green and cream — an effective, modernised version of the company's traditional livery. Also in 1996, M&D acquired the business and site of Mercury, based on the Isle of Grain, and in August 1997 bought some of the services and vehicles of Wealden-Beeline of Five Oak Green.

Following a boardroom shake-up, the Cowie group announced that it was to drop that name and re-brand its buses, car dealerships and fleet-hires as 'Arriva', which, according to *The Times* of 15 November 1997, 'would make the company seem dynamic [and] proactive, and [would] appeal to women for psychological reasons'. It was announced that a new livery (turquoise and white) would be adopted nationwide (save in London) and local brand-names abolished, to 'save £300,000 on repainting buses that move between fleets'. Thus Invictaway was renamed Arriva Southern Counties, Kentish Bus became Arriva Kent Thameside [*sic*], and Company No 114841 — Maidstone & District Motor Services Ltd (registered in 1911) — Arriva Kent & Sussex Ltd. The Certificate of Change of Name was issued in April 1998. The M&D company still exists, but it isn't called that anymore!

▲ The Maidstone Park & Ride service — a contract awarded to M&D by the local borough council — was considerably enhanced from the winter of 1994/5 by the infusion of three new vehicles specifically dedicated to that task. Nos 3611-3 (M611-3 PKP) were Volvo B6 saloons with 40-seat Plaxton Pointer bodywork, selected from nine such vehicles delivered at that time. *Ian Allan Library*

▲ British Bus group purchased Maidstone & District in April 1995.
That group was, in turn, acquired by Cowie the following year.
The Cowie group opted to identify its subsidiary bus companies
individually, and a new Maidstone & District livery was designed
to go with a new M&D logo. No 5931 (P931 MKL), a Northern
Counties-bodied Volvo Olympian delivered in 1996, made an
all-too-brief appearance in these colours. *Arriva*

The Cowie group's
Maidstone & District
logo. *Arriva*

The Cowie group renamed itself 'Arriva' in November 1997. The decision was taken to dispense with individual company liveries and introduce a corporate identity nationally, together with its own new logo. The changes also put paid to the Maidstone & District name. This Mercedes-Benz midibus demonstrates; the legend upon its flanks now reads: 'ARRIVA serving the Medway Towns'.
Arriva

Further Reading

Among the sources I have found helpful and/or recommend for further reading are:

Books

'Bell Street' *East Surrey — The East Surrey Traction Co Ltd*, HJ Publications, 1974

Hibbs, John *The History of British Bus Services*, David & Charles, 1969

'Invicta' *The Tramways of Kent: Vol 1*, LRTL, 1974

Morris, Colin *History of British Bus Services: South East England*, TPC, 1980

Owen, Nicholas *History of the British Trolleybus*, David & Charles, 1974

M&D booklets

Hail and Farewell, to mark the conversion of trolleybus routes in Hastings and Bexhill to motorbus operation, 1959

50 Years of Service, 1961

M&D house magazines

The Green 'Un, 1930 onward

Inside Only, 1946 onward

Intercom (M&D and East Kent), 1974 onward

M&D News, 1985 onward

The Maidstone Traveller, 1997

For much greater detail, read:

The M&D Illustrated Fleet History 1911–1995, The M&D and East Kent Bus Club, 42 St Albans Hill, Hemel Hempstead HP3 9NG

and

'The Development of Motor Bus Services in North and West Kent from 1900 to 1936', papers by Richard E. Rosa, 77 Artillery Row, Gravesend DA12 1LY

Early in its operations, Maidstone & District used geographical tickets, specially printed for different routes, with the names of the stages printed down either side. They were cancelled by punching in the appropriate place. For some return journeys special tickets were printed, such as the white 2s 9d Chatham–Tenterden illustrated. Like many operators, Maidstone & District later switched to numbered stages; the pink 3d and yellow 6d are examples of this practice, which called for a much smaller range of tickets to be printed.

Over the years, Hastings & District and Chatham & District tended to follow similar practice to the parent company. The Hastings 1d is an example of a geographical ticket. The group's early tickets tended to be printed by Williamson of Ashton-under-Lyne, but it changed over to the Bell Punch Co, of London, in the 1930s.

At this time Maidstone & District changed to the Setright ticket machine, which stamped fare, date and stage number on a pre-printed ticket. The three companies followed similar practice. Illustrated here are a green Maidstone & District return, and a white exchange ticket, a yellow Chatham & District single, and a white Hastings Tramways worker's return. Bell Punch also printed special scholar's single tickets for the group; the example illustrated is from a block produced in the mid-1930s.

In the 1950s Maidstone & District changed over to the Setright Speed machine, which printed all the details on to smaller tickets issued from a single roll held inside the machine. Later still, the company adopted the Almex machine, issuing small square paper tickets. *Andrew Waller collection*